Segregation in Federally Subsidized Low-Income Housing in the United States

**Praeger Series in
Political Economy**
Rodney D. Green, Series Editor

Segregation in Federally Subsidized Low-Income Housing in the United States

Modibo Coulibaly,
Rodney D. Green, and
David M. James

Praeger Series in Political Economy

Westport, Connecticut
London

363.5850973
C 85 a

Library of Congress Cataloging-in-Publication Data

Coulibaly, Modibo.
    Segregation in federally subsidized low-income housing in the
United States / Modibo Coulibaly, Rodney D. Green, and David M.
James.
            p.   cm. — (Praeger series in political economy, ISSN
1072-2882)
    Includes bibliographical references and index.
    ISBN 0-275-94820-X (alk. paper)
    1. Discrimination in housing—United States.   2. Housing
subsidies—United States.   3. Segregation—United States.   4. Poor—
Housing—Government policy—United States.   I. Green, Rodney D.
II. James, David M.   III. Title.   IV. Series.
    HD7288.76.U5C68   1998
    363.5'85'0973—DC21   97-23347

British Library Cataloguing in Publication Data is available.

Library of Congress Catalog Card Number: 97-23347
ISBN: 0-275-94820-X
ISSN: 1072-2882

First published in 1998

Praeger Publishers, 88 Post Road West, Westport, CT 06881
An imprint of Greenwood Publishing Group, Inc.

Printed in the United States of America

The paper used in this book complies with the
Permanent Paper Standard issued by the National
Information Standards Organization (Z39.48-1984).

10   9   8   7   6   5   4   3   2   1

Contents

Tables

Preface

In the United States, low-income housing subsides are traditionally assumed to be a welfare program of income redistribution in favor of the poor, part of the social safety net designed to correct the apparent failure of the private housing market by providing decent housing at prices the poor can afford. It is moreover assumed that the long-term goal of low-income housing programs is to expand the housing opportunities of the poor.

In this study, we argue instead that despite formal claims of providing decent, safe, and sanitary housing for the poor, federal low-income housing programs have actually been used as instruments of urban renewal while accomplishing little to realize their formal goals. Born in the economic depression of the 1930s, low-income housing in the United States has been used to solve urban problems not directly related to the housing needs of the poor. And to the extent that low- and moderate-income families have received any housing assistance from the federal government, the benefits realized have been significantly depreciated by racial and income-based segregation in these programs. Although the levels have diminished since the civil rights movements of the 1960s, there still is significant segregation of subsidized housing tenants, both by race within and among housing projects and of the projects themselves from moderate- and high-income residential neighborhoods.

Following the introduction, beginning around 1960, of new forms of housing subsidy, such as those targeted to the elderly, public housing has increasingly been characterized by the concentration of African-Americans and other minority racial groups in high-density housing projects in inner city areas while whites predominate in scattered-site, low-density elderly housing projects located outside of the central city, patterns that seem beyond the influence of civil rights laws.

ACKNOWLEDGMENTS

This book was prepared under the auspices and with the support of the Center for Urban Progress at Howard University. We acknowledge with special thanks the support of John Goering of the U.S. Department of Housing and Urban Development for his stimulating comments and assistance in obtaining racial occupancy data for 1977 and 1992. We also owe special thanks to Dr. Emily Blank of the Department of Economics of Howard University for her helpful comments. For their assistance in obtaining historical and current data on subsidized low-income occupancy, we would like to thank Ms. Aloa South of the Civil Reference Branch of the National Archives in Washington, D.C., and Barbara Williams, Survey Statistician at the Bureau of the Census, American Housing Survey. We are also grateful to Dr. Mohamed Hassan for valuable assistance with data collection and data entry.

We would like to thank Professor Lawrence Gary, Director of the Institute for Urban Affairs and Research at Howard University, Dr. Orlando Taylor, Dean, and Dr. Johnnetta Davis, former Associate Dean, of the Howard University Graduate School of Arts and Science, for their encouragement and financial support, and Mrs. Geraldine Davis for typing several drafts of the original manuscript.

We owe a special gratitude to our wives, Kanny, Pauline, and Becky for supporting our efforts in completing this work.

1

Introduction

There have been many studies on the effects of segregation and economic inequality on education, income, wealth, social services, and housing in the United States. Such studies often assume, implicitly or explicitly, that segregation is a manifestation of generalized white prejudice resulting in discrimination against racial minorities, often mediated through an imperfect market mechanism. Following the passage of the Civil Rights Act in 1964, and the Fair Housing Act in 1968, it was widely believed that the new federal legislation would not only significantly remedy the inequalities resulting from this process by reducing segregation and stemming racial discrimination but also narrow the socioeconomic gap between racial groups. Fair housing would ultimately "turn this nation toward the creation of a slum-free, ghetto-free America [and] affect the whole pattern of urban housing and community life and actually lead to the establishment of fair housing throughout the United States."[1]

Some thirty years after these civil rights and fair housing initiatives, however, segregation continues to be a serious social and political challenge in most American cities. The failure of these initiatives is often attributed to the federal government's accommodation of local practices with regard to race relations or to a weak judicial and administrative enforcement of the Fair Housing Act. This study argues instead that segregation by race and income has been an integral element of the federal housing policy from its inception, and that subjective factors such as white prejudice and associated individual discrimination merely obscure the role of the federal government in creating and maintaining segregation. This proposition will be demonstrated through a historical and statistical review of federally subsidized low-rent housing.

FEDERAL HOUSING PROGRAMS: REDISTRIBUTION OR URBAN ACCOMMODATION?

Subsidized low-income housing in the United States is often assumed to be a welfare program of income redistribution in favor of the poor. In 1935, economist Frank Watson wrote,

a portion of our population receives an income too small to provide itself with what is considered a minimum of decent living quarters. An increase in wage levels can assist in this situation, but there will probably for some time to come always be a portion of our population whose services are of marginal economic value and who must consequently either enjoy standards of living not compatible with decency and health, or else have their costs of living borne in part at least by society in general. If the living standards of this group are to be raised, it must be done by a direct contribution from society. There is no way of providing decent housing for people who cannot afford decent housing.[2]

In fact, in the United States low-income housing became primarily an instrument of urban renewal rather than Watson's program of income redistribution. Even to the extent that low-income housing has been a program of income redistribution, its benefits have been depreciated by segregation and discrimination. As a result of segregation, racial minorities have often been denied units altogether or assigned exclusively to housing projects located in low-income neighborhoods with inferior services and amenities.[3]

This view is supported by the study that follows, in which we demonstrate that federally subsidized low-income housing in the United States has been, and continues to be, racially and economically segregated—despite the passage of landmark civil rights and fair housing legislation in the 1960s. While the particular findings of this study may be consistent with other interpretations of recent history, much collateral data, both systematic and anecdotal, suggest that the revisionist theoretical structure outlined here is useful in sorting out the contrast between the avowed purpose of these programs over six decades and their actual effects.

The principal issue can be summarized in two questions: What were the patterns and trends in both racial occupancy and income dispersal of subsidized housing projects during the period 1932–1992? Did these patterns and trends change as a result of the civil rights legislation of the 1960s?

Before the Civil Rights Act of 1964, segregation (at least racial segregation) was widely accepted, codified in some community laws, and the source of no noticeable opposition from federal housing agencies. The period from 1932, when the federal government first became involved in public housing construction and what was then called slum clearance), to the early 1960s, when discrimination and segregation in housing programs receiving direct or indirect federal financial aid were formally prohibited, will be referred to as the *early period of subsidized housing.*

The time since 1964, the high point of the civil rights movement with its important goal of ending segregation in the housing market, will be referred to as the *modern period of subsidized housing.* What distinguishes this period from the earlier one (at least formally) is the withdrawal of support for segregation by federal housing agencies. We hypothesize that during the early period, subsidized low-income housing projects were, as a matter of public policy, concentrated in low-income areas and assigned to tenants on the basis of race, and that this process still characterized the housing programs, with no significant improvement, in the modern period.

NOTES

1. National Committee Against Discrimination in Housing, *Citizens' Guide to the Federal Fair Housing Law of 1968* (New York: National Committee Against Discrimination in Housing, 1968), 12–13.

2. Frank Watson, *Housing Problems and Possibilities in the United States* (New York: Harper & Brothers, 1935), 16–17.

3. For similar examples, see Ann R. Markusen, "Class and Urban Social Expenditure: A Marxist Theory of Metropolitan Government," in *Marxism and the Metropolis: New Perspectives in Urban Political Economy*, ed. William K. Tabb and Larry Sawers, 2d ed. (New York: Oxford University Press, 1984), 82–100.

2

Housing, History, and Schools of Thought

In this section, we review concepts and analyses of residential segregation and housing market discrimination developed by various schools of thought. Racial residential segregation has rarely been analyzed in terms of objective relations of production, distribution, and exchange giving rise to segregation and public policies that support and reinforce it. Instead, most analyses have considered only formal, sometimes merely superficial, relationships between patterns of settlement and subjective beliefs and attitudes. More recently, the historical urban modeling work of David Gordon provides promising approaches for a more comprehensive study of housing segregation.

THE EARLY PERIOD (BEFORE 1964)

Before the Civil War, racial segregation in the United States was ironically not a major social problem.[1] With the end of slavery, however, the question of how to assimilate free blacks into mainstream society became a thorny political and social issue.[2] In an address delivered in Peoria in 1854, Abraham Lincoln summarized what would become post-slavery conventional wisdom:

Free them, and make them politically and socially our equal? My own feelings will not admit of this; and if mine would, we well know that those of the great masses of white people will not. Whether this feeling accords with justice and sound judgment, is not the sole question, if indeed, it is any part of it. A universal feeling whether well or ill founded cannot be safely disregarded. We cannot, then, make them equals.[3]

Over the next century the alleged opposition of the "great masses of white people" to the political and economic progress of free blacks may not have been as irrational as Lincoln implied. Black workers could become an economic threat to white workers, if used by employers to break the strikes and undermine the economic demands of organized white labor.[4] Employers found black workers more tractable than white workers, and hence useful tools in battles for lower labor costs and against union activities. As Sumner Eliot describes, Reconstruction-era employers,

in order to keep wages down and prevent the unions from getting too strong, did not actually have to bring in Negro workers. Sometimes just rumors of the possibility of such action served the same purpose, and thus constituted a threat to the labor movement. Imagine what must have been the feelings of the New England workers upon reading a report from the Washington correspondent of the *Boston Post* to the effect that the organization of an emigration society was being contemplated for the purpose of shipping to the manufacturing centers of New England 200,000 to 300,000 able-bodied Negro workers, who, it was said, would help lower the cost of labor. The [April 3, 1866] *Boston Daily Evening Voice*, a leading labor paper, reprinted the story and commented that such an eventuality was exactly what papers such as the *Post* wished, and exactly what the workers would see if they were not careful.[5]

The social restrictions placed on free blacks were thus far from irrational; they were perceived by many whites (correctly or not) as a safeguard of their own economic security.[6] Labor historian Gerald Grob notes that the issue of race became "even more acute after the Civil War, when emancipation threw the Negro worker into more direct competition with his white counterpart. As a result white workers made systematic and repeated attempts to bar or segregate Negroes and keep them out of unions. Employers were also quick to exploit the issue of race to prevent unionizing activities, especially in the South."[7]

Nevertheless, mainstream social scientists of the late nineteenth and early twentieth centuries usually attributed the social condition of free blacks to "racial prejudice"—itself often assumed to spring naturally from innate biological differences among different species of humankind.[8] To disregard prevailing white prejudices and attempt to improve the social and economic "conditions of Negroes," a popular theme went, would be fruitless.[9] According to Robert Parks, as long as the "Negro remains in his place" (a place assigned him by traditions of racial hierarchy), race relations would cause little friction or comment. "It is when the Negro invades a new region that race riots occur; it is when he seeks a place in a new occupation or a new profession that he meets the most vigorous opposition; it is when he seeks to assume a new dignity that he ceases to be quaint and becomes ridiculous."[10]

For Parks the "Negro" had been assigned a definite place in the "social order," and "race prejudice has made it difficult for him to get out of it."[11]

Existing class relations of production, distribution, and exchange were ana-lytically irrelevant to Parks's understanding of race relations.[12] Many other early twentieth-century observers of race relations similarly minimized or ignored labor-market competition between black and white workers (often deliberately created by employers) as a factor in race riots and other forms of conflict in industrial cities, preferring instead to view such events as conflicts between inevitably antagonistic racial groups. These antagonisms were some-times even blamed on ill-thought-out immigration laws which unintention-ally encouraged an influx of racially biased foreigners.[13] According to a nativist account published in the Detroit *Tribune*, the 1895 race riot of Spring Valley, Illinois, was caused by Italians

who are still so un-American that they require to have the mayor's address interpreted to them. [These Italians] have taken it upon themselves to say that no colored man, born upon the soil, shall work or even live in that community. We are told in the dispatches that "The foreign element, which dominates the situation, declares that no man, black or white, shall return to work until the coal company agrees to discharge every colored man in its employ, and also to hire no new men of either race; that all idle men"—whom they approve—"in Spring Valley shall be given employment." This is their modest demand. What country is this anyway? Can this be America, "the land of the free and the home of the brave?" Is it possible that there is law in Illinois, and peace officers, and a militia, and a governor? Aye! there's the rub! Illinois has a gov-ernor, but someway the impression has gone out, since he pardoned the Haymarket anarchists, that his sympathies are not strong for law and order.[14]

By 1929, deepening economic strains had produced a large-scale housing crisis. In most cities, few low- or moderate-income families of any race could afford decent housing. Such families tended to be concentrated in central-city areas, while most higher-income citizens dispersed to concentric rings around the central city.

To explain these settlement patterns—aggravated and made more visible by the Depression—social scientists began to examine factors other than preju-dice. Among the first researchers to broaden the scope of the study of racial residential segregation were those of the urban ecology school of Ernest Bur-gess. In 1928, Burgess asserted that "the residential separation of white and Negro has almost invariably been treated by itself as if it was a unique phe-nomenon of urban life. In fact, however, . . . this is only one case among many of the working of the process of segregation in the sorting and shifting of the different elements of population in the growth of the city."[15]

According to Burgess, the immigrant colonies—the Jewish ghettos, little Sicilies, and Chinatowns, as well as the black belt (i.e., the homogeneous urban black ghetto)—were essentially low-income zones inhabited by eco-nomically disadvantaged people. For Burgess, the existence of different in-come areas in cities and their accompanying ethnic specificity could be attributed to the distribution of income. Urban ecologists maintained that cit-ies have a typical residential configuration, that beneath the "surface confusion of any city's life," there are definite and objective patterns of settlement of households with different levels of income. "As we study residential segregation," wrote Harvey Zorbaugh in 1938, "we find that from city to city they conform to a typical pattern of *segregation*—a typical ecological distribution of physical and social features. This basic segregation is in broad zones about the central business district—a transitional or slum zone; a zone of working men's homes; a middle-class residential zone; and beyond, a commuting zone of communities of higher economic status."[16]

Although urban ecologists correctly stressed that factors like the distribution of income were critical for a better understanding of urban residential settlement, they seldom examined segregation by income and race as a historically contingent form of urban settlement.

The limitation of the ecological analysis led some observers to propose alternative, class-based explanations of urban residential segregation. In *Patterns of Negro Segregation*, published in 1943, Charles Johnson defines the problem of racial residential segregation in terms of the "class and caste division of the society." Johnson uses the term *class* not in its Marxist definition based on the ownership of the means of productions, but to refer to social groups deliberately created by the ruling elite in its attempt to conceal the nature of society from the oppressed masses. He wrote,

When the middle class became the custodian of democracy immediately following the Civil War, it ushered in an insistent capitalism which demanded a society no less stratified than the one which it had conquered. Capitalism could be fully realized only if the masses, who were not to share in the larger economic benefits emanating from it, could be pacified in the meantime. The solution was reached by providing the masses with an illusion of superiority in relation to a lower caste, the Negro group, and thus obscuring for a time the undemocratic tendencies of the total pattern of society. It is against this background of class and caste struggle, of a democracy defensive against the economic processes within its framework, that Negro segregation and discrimination must be studied and analyzed.[17]

Using this class and caste framework, Johnson argues that the pattern of "Negro segregation" can be predicted from the character of the "dominant economy." Thus, in the North, where "free market" capitalism was the dominant mode of production and distribution, spatial segregation of "Negro" and white workers became the established pattern of settlement, consistent with a (probably false) belief that residential segregation helps to reduce racial conflicts.[18] In the South, continues Johnson, where the dominant economy was "semi-feudal," a "back-yard pattern of Negro segregation" became necessary to accommodate people who "could afford a Negro maid."[19]

Following Johnson, some later proponents of the class and caste analysis of residential segregation argued that the role of subjective factors in explaining segregation was minimal and that, indeed, subjective prejudice and public policy are ultimately subordinated to the needs of the dominant economic interests. For instance, William Julius Wilson wrote in 1978 that "in the preindustrial and industrial [modern] periods the basis of structured racial inequality was primarily economic, and in most situations the state was merely an instrument to reinforce patterns of race relations that grew directly out of the social relations of production."[20]

Indeed, racial residential segregation was often reinforced by immediate economic motives of landlords and developers who sought to maximize their real estate profits by catering to the perceived prejudices of their higher-income customers (who were, of course, white).[21] Such motives can also be seen in elements of a national housing policy of the late 1930s and 1940s designed to protect property values against "undesirable encroachment" and racially "inharmonious use."[22] Like any private entrepreneur, the author of this policy, the newly created Federal Housing Administration (FHA), was chiefly interested in financial success. Prejudice and discrimination became part of public policy so that profit could be made.[23]

W. E. B. Du Bois and Other Black Intellectuals

W. E. B. Du Bois and other African-American intellectuals presented much deeper analyses of race relations and racial segregation in the United States than those of Johnson or the urban ecologists. Although Du Bois assumed that subjective prejudice in itself plays an important role in explaining race relations in America, he also sought to link interracial friction to deliberate policies of the white establishment, motivated by profits, to "exploit and oppress members" of the black race.[24] Du Bois argued that slavery, for example, was purely "a matter of economics," a question of income and labor rather than a problem of "right and wrong or the physical differences in men." Once the system of slavery became the source of substantial income for "men and nations," a "frantic search for moral and racial justification" ensued.[25] Du Bois noted in 1947 that "After the Civil War, there was still prospect of tremendous post war profits on cotton and other products of Southern agriculture. Therefore, what the North wanted was not freedom and higher wages for black labor, but its control under such forms of law as would keep it cheap; and also stop its open competition with Northern labor. The moral protest of abolitionists must be appeased, but profitable industry was determined to control wages and governments."[26]

Du Bois's critique, however, tended to be narrow in focus. Racial segregation was defined and analyzed not in the context of a social system of production and distribution but as a product of an orchestrated conspiracy of the "White Man" against "the Negro race."[27] Consequently, to defeat this conspiracy, the "Negro race" was urged to unite and to be "collectively self-reliant." The historian Newell Sims followed this line of thought when he wrote in "Techniques of Race Adjustment" in 1931 that

The Negro's procedure calls for a concentration and direction of his group resources with a view to using them to the advantage of his group and to the enhancing of its power as rapidly as possible. If and when this is done the Negro will be in a position where he will no longer have to beg for justice and opportunity to pursue life and happiness as he likes but will be able to exact justice and command opportunity. There is much idle talk about the Negro's rights and about America's obligation to him, but actually in the minds of the majority of white Americans, the Negro has no rights and America has no obligations toward him. This is the realistic aspect of the situation. If then he is to enjoy rights, he must win them by his own efforts, and if America acknowledges any obligations to him, it will be only as he compels it. It is largely in this spirit, I take it, that the program of the National Association for the Advancement of Colored People has been conceived.[28]

Mainstream Analyses, 1940–1960

After the Great Depression and World War II, analyses of racial residential segregation broadened. For Arnold Rose and Will Maslow, among others, psychological explanations of racial conflict were no longer adequate.[29] In "Prejudice, Discrimination, and the Law," published in 1951, Maslow rhetorically questions the logic of prevailing psychological explanations of race relations, arguing that

Attitudes do not automatically flower into behavior, and that whether or not a prejudiced person acts in accordance with his beliefs depends on many factors, not the least of which is the community's notion of what is right and proper. Northerners are prone to regard the South as one undifferentiated mass of bigotry. Such a conclusion is of course preposterous. The best demonstration of its falsity is the elaborate *legal* measures designed by the southern lawmaker to create and reinforce prejudice. If everyone in the South looked at the Negro with contempt and revulsion, it would not be necessary to enact laws (and occasionally to punish violators) forbidding racial intermarriage and rigorously commanding the separation of Negro and white. Southern Jim Crow laws are designed to whip the rebel, the nonconformist, and the laggard in line [emphasis added].[30]

Despite such skepticism, subjective prejudice and attitudes remained pivotal in orthodox analyses of racial segregation, and segregation, as a rule, continued to be studied with little or no reference to its systemic context. In *An American Dilemma*, for example, Gunnar Myrdal describes the "Negro problem" in the United States as a vicious social cycle.[31] At any time, Myrdal argues, the social position of black people is determined by existing white attitudes and behaviors. Most whites regard blacks with revulsion because of their "poverty, slum dwelling, superstition, dirty appearance, criminality, disorderly conduct, etc."[32] This in itself could lower the economic standard of living of blacks and make them culturally more distinct from the white population; as this happens, fewer and fewer whites would be inclined to associate themselves with blacks. Thus, following Myrdal, the level of white prejudice increases. This vicious cycle of declining standards of living of blacks and escalating white prejudice, according to Myrdal, could perpetuate itself ad infinitum.[33]

Myrdal's cycle could operate in the opposite direction as well. If, as the result of "a philanthropic gift," blacks succeed in improving their standards of living (which are assumed to be universally low), they could thereby lower the level of white prejudice, which in turn would permit a higher "Negro plane of living." This cycle of improving standards of living of blacks and declining white prejudice would also continue, in theory, ad infinitum, or at least as long as vestiges of white prejudice remain in society.[34]

Myrdal makes no reference in his analysis to such phenomena in the history of race relations as the deliberate use and aggravation of racial animosities by employers in labor disputes. He also does not explain why "Negro poverty, superstition, and ignorance" should elicit a special white prejudice in a society in which members of other racial and ethnic groups, including whites, were equally poor and ignorant, or why the economic uplift of the black population should be a matter of pure altruism.

While Myrdal's analysis was typical of mainstream views of race relations, treating "white prejudice," independent of any systemic economic context, as the primary cause of racial residential segregation, two other perspectives are worthy of note.

One is that of the urban ecologists who—having observed, from city to city, that patterns of residential settlement in general were closely correlated with income distribution—saw racial segregation as simply part of a general trend toward the residential separation of households by income. However, they seldom examined the social contexts that generated and perpetuated this distribution.

Yet other researchers, including Johnson, proposed explanations for segregation based on the explicit recognition that society is divided into "classes and castes." In this class and caste analysis of segregation the "Negro race" as a whole was lower class. Social divisions within the lower class itself were assumed not to be germane to racial residential segregation. The Negro, according to Johnson, was deliberately kept at the bottom of the social ladder by a ruling elite eager to conceal the real nature of society from the masses.

Nevertheless, perspectives such as Myrdal's—that the position of blacks in society is determined by the level of white prejudice and that blacks would improve their social and economic conditions only insofar as they succeed in reducing the level of white prejudice—dominated most analysis from World War II until the 1960s.

CIVIL RIGHTS AND BEYOND

Mainstream Analyses

In the 1960s, amid intense civil turmoil, researchers found that the impact of race on property value was minimal, contrary to conventional wisdom. Findings that the movement of outsiders into a racially homogeneous (usually all white) neighborhood did not diminish but could, in fact, increase the

value of existing properties undermined a basic rationale for housing discrimination and deed restrictions, although they by no means gave the *coup
de grâce* to nonsystemic explanations of race relations.[35]

Neoclassical economists, whose ideas were based on "the sphere of simple
circulation or exchange of commodities," launched a new, limited hedonic
view of race relations.[36] In a seminal 1957 work, Gary Becker averred,

In analyzing discrimination in the marketplace, individuals are assumed to act as if
they have "tastes for discrimination" and these tastes are the most important immediate cause of actual discrimination. [Therefore,] money, commonly used as a measuring rod, will also serve as a measure of discrimination. If an individual has a 'taste for
discrimination,' he must act *as if* he were willing to pay something either directly or in
the form of a reduced income, to be associated with some persons instead of others.
When actual discrimination occurs, he must, in fact, either pay or forfeit income for
this privilege. This *simple way of looking at the matter gets at the essence of prejudice
and discrimination* [emphasis added].[37]

Becker's perspective continues to be embraced by many researchers, despite much criticism,[38] and has deepened the focus on exogenously generated
individual prejudices as the cause of racial inequality.

Some students of race relations consider skin color to be a significant factor in explaining racial segregation for entirely different reasons from those
of Becker.[39] According to Karl Taeuber, "An extensive literature on prejudice
and discrimination suggests the relevance of the visibility of a group to the
perceived threat it arouses. Regardless of specific behavioral mechanisms,
there is ample reason to expect the relative size of a minority population to be
related to its social position."[40]

Taeuber simulated different income distribution models among black and
white residents of Cleveland and concluded that "altering income distribution without eliminating discrimination would only tend to increase segregation. Income improvements or housing subsidies enable additional white
families to emulate the segregated residential patterns enjoyed by middle and
higher income whites. Such programs enable Negro families to seek improved
housing, but the search must be conducted within the confines of a tightly
segregated housing market."[41]

To effectively reduce racial residential segregation, Taeuber concluded, the
barriers of "white prejudice and discrimination" in the housing market must
be removed:

Allow the family income distribution of whites and Negroes to remain fixed. Hypo-
thetically remove racial discrimination and any other race-connected factors that affect housing choice among low-income families. Assume that anti-discrimination
policies are not effective among high income families, who continue to maintain segregated residential patterns. [The] resulting white–Negro segregation index would be
10. In other words, the great bulk of the problem of racial residential segregation

would be solved if the housing of middle-income and poor families were integrated, even though segregation persisted among high-income families.[42]

Taeuber's study later became the empirical justification for rejecting the economic explanations of racial residential segregation pioneered by urban ecologists. Pettigrew, for example, wrote in 1979 that it is a "comforting misconception" to assume that racial segregation can be explained by differential racial incomes similar to the patterns of residential separation between social class groups. At the same time, however, Pettigrew appears to be suggesting that the spatial settlement of blacks, similar to the spatial settlement of other racial and ethnic groups, varies with economic status.[43] "Younger, educated black families," Pettigrew argues, can "buy new homes in the suburbs" or live on the "outer boundaries of the ghetto."[44] They are a group of "people whom middle-class white suburbanites are generally willing to greet as neighbors."[45] By contrast, the poorly educated and financially afflicted blacks are still largely confined to the "central black areas in the core city." The patterns of settlement, in short, "mirror the diverging socioeconomic developments among blacks. As these processes proceed, a geographical as well as socioeconomic distance is likely to develop between the two status poles of the black world. Such a development is, of course, comparable to that of the white world."[46]

The same conflicting arguments can be found in *Contemporary Urban Ecology* by Brian Berry and John Kasarda. First, the authors argue that "for the bulk of white Americans" race plays an important role in ascribing "neighborhood status, even after education, income and occupational levels are considered."[47] Later, however, they discuss a "significant trend" toward the "separation of socioeconomic groups," that is, the separation of people with "different income, education, and occupational levels."[48]

Mainstream analyses of segregation are inconsistent. Although racial segregation in its manifestation is maintained by strong economic forces, mainstream analysts assume that it is rooted in human nature. Specific economic causes of segregation, such as property values and their associated effect on the profitability of the real estate market, the distribution of household income (purchasing power), and access to public services, are, as a rule, considered to be secondary to the psychological causes. This approach is exculpatory since it tends to shift the blame for racial residential segregation to individuals and, thereby, diffuses and confuses the causes of a social system of racial segregation.

Quantitative Measurements of Segregation

While post–World War II writers held analytically limited views on the source of racial discrimination in housing and its functional role in a social system of production, distribution, and exchange, they nevertheless developed reasonable tools of analysis for conducting empirical evaluation of the presence or absence of segregation. Among these, the index D of residential dissimilarity is the most frequently used. It is calculated by the following formula (assuming two racial groups, blacks and whites):

$$D = \frac{1}{2} \sum_{i}^{n} |\, w_{1i} - w_{2i} \,| \, 100 \qquad\qquad (1)$$

where D is the index of residential dissimilarity, w_{1i} is the ith tract's share of the city's black population and w_{2i} is the ith tract's share of the city's white population.

The value of the index D varies between 0 and 100. If each tract in the city contains only whites or only blacks, then the spatial distribution of the racial groups is as uneven as possible, and "the value of the index will be maximized and equal to 100."[49] On the other hand, if each tract has "each group represented in the same proportion" of its total population as in the city as a whole then the value of the index is the minimum, 0. In this case, the distribution of racial groups is as even as possible and there is no "racial residential segregation."[50]

Despite its popularity, the dissimilarity index has some limitations. Since racial segregation is defined in terms of the distribution of groups in space, any absence of evenness in this distribution is subsumed under *racial segregation*. In particular, the index of residential dissimilarity makes no provision for voluntary racial associations in space. The index also suffers from other problems.[51]

The limitations of the index of residential dissimilarity led to the introduction of alternative measures of racial segregation, including Michael White's indices P_{xx} of proximity and P of segregation.[52] As with the index D of dissimilarity, the index P of proximity is a measure of spatial distribution of racial groups, indicating the extent to which tracts inhabited by minority members adjoin one another in space.[53]

A third measure of racial segregation is the index of exposure introduced by Stanley Lieberson.[54] Exposure refers to the "degree of potential contact, or the possibility of interaction, between minority group members within geographic areas of a city."[55]

Other less frequently used measures of racial segregation include the *index of concentration*, which measures the amount of "physical space occupied by a minority group"; the *index of clustering*, which measures the concentration of the distribution of a minority group in the city; and the *index of centralization*, which measures the degree to which members of a minority group tend to congregate toward the central city core. These empirical measures have a certain usefulness as indicators of static conditions, but their abstractness limits their analytical scope. A more holistic approach is needed.

Urban Development and Residential Segregation

Many mainstream analyses of racial residential segregation are based on the presumed predilection of whites as a whole to prefer spatially segregated patterns of settlement. Racial segregation is implicitly assumed to be a vicious social cycle in which positive interracial contacts likely to change human predilections cannot be cultivated because of segregation.[56]

In 1984, an alternative analysis of urban segregation was introduced by David Gordon. Originally, Gordon set out to show the relationships between stages of development of American cities and the process of capital accumulation, and to show that qualitatively different methods of capital accumulation require qualitatively distinct forms of urban residential settlement.[57]

Gordon argued that, in the United States, urban forms could be classified into three historical types depending on the dominant form of capital accumulation (the *commercial city* of merchant capitalism; the *industrial city* of competitive industrial capitalism; and the *corporate city* of monopoly—corporate—capitalism)[58] each with a definite and distinct pattern of residential settlement of income groups emerging from class relations.[59]

In the commercial city of early merchant capitalism, the distribution of the population among residential locations was essentially random and cultural:

Most families owned their own property and acted as independent economic agents. Most establishments remained small, making it possible for nearly everyone to live and work in the same place. People from many different backgrounds and occupations were interspersed throughout the central city districts, with little obvious socioeconomic residential segregation. . . . Only one group failed to share in this central port-district life. Poor itinerants—beggars, casual seamen, propertyless laborers—all lived outside the cities, huddling in shanties and rooming houses.[60]

Because of British-imposed limits on colonial trade, the commercial city did not become a geographically widespread urban form in the United States but remained concentrated in a relatively limited area. It was nevertheless significant. Between 1790 and 1810, 45 percent of the urban population in the United States was in the four cities of Philadelphia, New York, Boston, and Baltimore.[61]

The development in the nineteenth century of manufacturing capitalism led to the replacement of the commercial city by the industrial city. In its pure form, according to Gordon, the industrial city was dominated by factories and plants in industrial districts near rail and water outlets. The first urban form was oriented toward trade and other mercantile activities; the later urban form served the needs of large-scale industrial production.

The residential settlement of the industrial city exhibited heterogeneous patterns. Near factories and plants were "entirely segregated working-class housing districts" crammed densely together. These districts contained tenement housing in cities like New York and row houses in cities such as Philadelphia. "Whatever the specific features of the housing, it was typically clustered together in isolation from middle and upper classes."[62] Higher-income people and their families began to move away from the densely populated central city to the periphery of the urban area. The wealthy and not-so-wealthy joined in this "fleeing from the noise and confusion of the waterfront, the dirt, the stench, and the intolerably crowded conditions of the old central city."[63]

In sum, according to Gordon, the settlement of industrial cities was in "successive concentric rings moving along the transport spokes radiating from the center." In the center of the city were shopping districts providing "centralized shopping outlets on which the middle and upper classes could converge for their marketing."[64] Like that of the commercial city, the development of the industrial city was uneven across the nation, the process advancing the most in the North, while remaining relatively embryonic in the South and West.

In the twentieth century, the monopolistic consolidation of economic power and intensifying labor disputes led to the development of the corporate city. In the North, where the industrial city was mature, the transition to the corporate city was accomplished through the transformation of downtown shopping districts and near-downtown areas, residential or industrial, into "downtown central business districts, dominated by skyscrapers."[65] Surrounding these central business districts "were emptying manufacturing areas, depressed from the desertion of large plants, barely surviving on the light and competitive industries left behind. Next to those districts were the old working-class districts, often transformed into ghettos locked into the cycle of central-city manufacturing decline."[66]

In the South and West, where the industrial city had not truly developed, the corporate city was developed "from scratch." "These became the exemplary corporate cities. They could be constructed from scratch to fit the needs of a new period of accumulation in which factory plant and equipment were themselves increasingly predicated upon a decentralized model."[67]

Like its predecessors, the corporate city appears fixed and unyielding. Over a much longer horizon, however, it seems more contingent. As the development of capitalism becomes more global with multinational corporations ranging the globe in search of profitable places of investment, the corporate city may be replaced by yet other urban forms.

Gordon succeeded in describing the process of urban residential settlement in its systemic context of capitalism far better than the urban ecologists. The analysis shows the limited power that subjective beliefs and attitudes have on the pattern of urban settlement, and how significant the role of public policy can be. The historical work of Gordon explains why residential differentiation cannot be fully understood by merely alluding to autonomous and spontaneous individual preferences. Perhaps David Harvey said it best, "there is a scale of action at which the individual loses control of the social conditions of existence in the face of forces mobilized through the capitalist production process. . . . It is at this boundary that individuals come to sense their own helplessness in the face of forces that do not appear amenable . . . even to collective political mechanisms of control."[68]

A surprising limitation of Gordon's work, however, is his meager discussion of race and ethnicity. Although he often refers to "ethnic segregation" and to a reserve "army of the unemployed-jobless workers available for immediate employment" whose existence would "help discipline those inside the factory gates," he does not examine the racial makeup of this reserve army of labor or discuss the implications for residential settlement of a racially divided workforce. (Some efforts in this direction are contained in Green's 1984 study of antebellum Richmond, Virginia.)[69] Meanwhile, Robert Weaver observed in 1950 that

The color line in employment was well entrenched in the United States by 1929. The whole economic, political and social structure of the South dictated and supported it. In the North, long experience with importation of Negro strikebreakers had created anti-Negro sentiment on the part of the white workers. Institutionalized racial segregation in the South and spatial segregation in the North supported these attitudes. In all parts of the nation, the black worker had become a symbol of a potential threat to the white worker. This fear had grown out of the American worker's experience with an economy which has seldom had enough jobs to absorb the labor supply.[70]

SUMMARY OF THE POST–CIVIL RIGHTS LITERATURE

After World War II, despite a growing theoretical and empirical challenge, mainstream explanations of urban residential segregation continued to be based on psychological factors. For some neoclassical economists, race relations, like any other commodity, are determined by individual tastes and invisible market forces. For others, the visibility of racial minorities and whites' fears of status loss were at the root of racial residential segregation; improving the economic conditions of racial minorities (particularly blacks) without eliminating these race-connected barriers to integration could, in Taeuber's view, increase segregation.

For David Gordon, urban residential segregation, at least in its economic dimension, can best be understood and analyzed in the context of capitalism and capital accumulation; qualitative changes in the method of capital accumulation lead to qualitative changes in the pattern of urban spatial settlement. In the commercial city, the small scale of economic operations allowed residential settlement patterns to be essentially random. As the scale of production and capital accumulation increased in industrial and corporate cities, qualitatively different patterns of residential segregation based on economic status of various groups emerged. Like those of the urban ecologists, Gordon's model of segregation arrays residential neighborhoods in concentric zones around the central business district with distance of each neighborhood from the center related to the income of its residents. Unlike the urban ecologists, Gordon takes some account of the deeper economic patterns driving these income distributions.

NOTES

1. Social problems, according to Arnold Rose, are situations that affect "a large number of people and when there is a consensus that there is a problem and that something can be done to alleviate it." Arnold M. Rose, "Theory for the Study of Social Problems," *Social Problems* 4, 3 (1957): 190; see also *International Encyclopedia of the Social Sciences*, 1972 ed., s.v. "Social Problem."

2. "The treatment of black Americans," wrote Thomas Pettigrew, "has been a national issue since our beginning; it has been persistently our key domestic issue of conflict; and it has shaped and contorted much of our social structure." Thomas F. Pettigrew, "Racial Change and Social Policy," *The Annals of the American Academy of Political and Social Sciences* 441 (1979): 115.

3. John Hope Franklin, "The Two Worlds of Race: A Historical View," in *The Negro American*, edited and with an introduction by Talcott Parsons and Kenneth B. Clark (Boston: Houghton Mifflin, 1966). 53.

4. According to a white UMW member, "as far as we are concerned as miners, the colored men are with us in the mines. They work side by side with us. They are members of our organization; can receive as much consideration from the officials of the organization as any other members, no matter what color. We treat them that way. . . . There is only one particular objection, and that is they are used to a great extent in being taken from one place to another to break a strike." W. E. B. Du Bois, "The Negro Artisan," *Report of a Social Study made under the Direction of Atlanta University; Together with the Proceedings of the Seventh Conference for the Study of the Negro Problems, Held at Atlanta University, May 27, 1902*, ed. W. E. B. Du Bois, (Atlanta: Atlanta University Press, 1902), 161.

5. Sumner Eliot, "The Labor Movement and the Negro During Reconstruction," *Journal of Negro History* 33, 4 (1948): 429–430; see also Charles S. Johnson, "Some Aspects of Negro Migration," *Opportunity* (October 1927): 297–299.

6. For a discussion, see Charles H. Wesley, *Negro Labor in the United States 1850–1925* (New York: Vanguard, 1927); Eliot, "The Labor Movement and the Negro," 426–468 passim; Daphne Spain, "Race Relations and Residential Segregation in New Orleans: Two Centuries of Paradox," *The Annals of the American Academy of Political and Social Sciences* 441 (1979): 82–96.

7. Gerald N. Grob, "Organized Labor and the Negro Worker, 1865–1900," *Labor History* 1, 2 (1960): 164.

8. "In looking for an explanation of the antipathy which one race feels toward another, we may first of all inquire whether there are any conditions arising in the course of the biological development of a species which, aside from social activities, leads to a predilection for those of one's own kind and a prejudice against organically different groups. And we do, in fact, find such conditions." William L. Thomas, "The Psychology of Race Prejudice," *American Journal of Sociology* 9 (1904): 593.

9. See, for example, Robert Parks, "The Bases of Race Prejudice," *The Annals of the American Academy of Political and Social Sciences* 140 (1928): 11–20.

10. Ibid., 15.

11. Ibid.

12. For a critique of similar psychological explanations of race relations, see Ira Katznelson, *City Trenches: Urban Politics and the Patterning of Class in the United States* (New York: Pantheon, 1981).

13. Philip S. Foner and Ronald L. Lewis, eds. *The Black Worker: A Documentary History from Colonial Times to the Present*, vol. 4, *The Black Worker during the Era of the American Federation of Labor and the Railroad Brotherhood* (Philadelphia: Temple University Press, 1979), 204–205; "The Massacre of East St Louis: An Investigation by the National Association for the Advancement of Colored People," *The Crisis* (September 1917): 219–238.

14. Foner and Lewis, *The Black Worker*, 4: 205.

15. Ernest W. Burgess, "Residential Segregation in American Cities," *The Annals of the American Academy of Political and Social Sciences* 140 (November 1928): 105; T. J. Woofter, *Negro Problems in Cities* (Garden City, N.Y.: Doubleday Doran, 1928), Chapter 3 passim.

16. Harvey W. Zorbaugh, "Urban Growth and Urban Planning," in *Public Housing Management: A Course of Lectures Offered by the New York University Division of General Education in Cooperation with the Municipal Service Commission and the New York Housing Authority* (New York: New York University Library, 1938), 8.

17. Charles S. Johnson, *Patterns of Negro Segregation* (New York: Harper & Brothers, 1943), xvii; see also Charles S. Johnson, "The Economic Status of Negroes," in *Summary and Analysis of the Materials Presented at the Conference on the Economic Status of the Negro, Held in Washington, D.C., May 11–13, 1933 under the Sponsorship of the Julius Rosenwald Fund,* prepared by Charles S. Johnson (Nashville: Fiske University Press, 1933).

18. Ibid., 203.

19. Ibid., 202.

20. William Julius Wilson, *The Declining Significance of Race: Blacks and Changing American Institutions* (Chicago: University of Chicago Press, 1978), 150.

21. Herman H. Long and Charles S. Johnson, *People v. Property: Race Restrictive Covenants in Housing* (Nashville: Fisk University Press, 1947); Charles S. Johnson, *To Stem This Tide: A Survey of Racial Tension Areas in the United States* (New York: Pilgrim Press, 1943); Robert C. Weaver, "Race Restrictive Housing Covenants," *Journal of Land & Public Utility Economics* 20, 3 (1944): 183–193; Benjamin R. Epstein and Arnold Foster, "Discrimination in Housing," in *Minority Problems in the United States: A Textbook of Readings in Intergroup Relations*, ed. Arnold M. Rose and Caroline B. Rose (New York: Harper & Row, 1965), 166–175; see also Robert C. Weaver, *The Negro Ghetto* (New York: Russell & Russell, 1948).

22. The *Underwriting Manual of the Federal Housing Administration* contains instructions and regulations to be followed by the underwriting staff. It lists "protection" that must be taken against "adverse influences." Where little or no protection is provided against "adverse influences," the valuator is instructed not to "hesitate to make a reject rating of this feature." Federal Housing Administration, *The Underwriting Manual* (Washington, D.C., 1938), 935; see also Homer Hoyt, *The Structure and Growth of Residential Neighborhoods in American Cities* (Washington, D.C.: Federal Housing Administration, 1939).

23. Charles Abrams, *Forbidden Neighbors: A Study of Prejudice in Housing* (New York: Harper & Brothers, 1955), Chapter 16.

24. Langston Hughes, "Merry-Go-Around," *Common Ground* (Spring 1942): 27.

25. W. E. B. Du Bois, "Three Centuries of Discrimination Against the Negro," in *Minority Problems in the United States: A Textbook of Readings in Intergroup Relations,* ed. Arnold M. Rose and Caroline B. Rose (New York: Harper & Row, 1965), 19.

26. Ibid., 22–23.

27. Ralph Ellison, *The Invisible Man* (New York: Vintage Books, 1947).

28. Newell L. Sims, "Techniques of Race Adjustment," *Journal of Negro History* 16, 1 (1931): 84.

29. Arnold M. Rose, "Intergroup Relations v. Prejudice: A Pertinent Theory for the Study of Social Change," *Social Problems* 4, 2 (1956): 173–176.

30. Will Maslow, "Prejudice, Discrimination, and the Law," *The Annals of the American Academy of Political and Social Sciences* 275 (1951): 9–17.

31. Gunnar Karl Myrdal, *An American Dilemma* (New York: Harper & Brothers, 1944), 1066.

32. Ibid.

33. Ibid.

34. Ibid., 1067.

35. See, for example, Luigi Laurenti, *Property Value and Race: Studies in Seven Cities* (Berkeley and Los Angeles: University of California Press, 1960); Davis McEntire, *Residence and Race* (Berkeley and Los Angeles: University of California Press, 1960).

36. Karl Marx, *Capital: A Critique of Political Economy*, vol. 1, part 2 (Moscow: Progress Publishers, 1978).

37. Gary S. Becker, *The Economics of Discrimination*, 2d ed. (Chicago: University of Chicago Press, 1957), 6. As noted by David Harvey, "bourgeois ideology and politics typically seek to forge a consciousness favorable to the perpetuation of the capitalist order and actively seek out ways to draw social distinctions along lines other than that between capital and labor." See David Harvey, *The Urbanization of Capital: Studies in the History and Theory of Capitalist Urbanization* (Baltimore: Johns Hopkins University Press, 1985): 116.

38. Suzanne M. Bianchi, Reynolds Farley, and Daphne Spain, "Racial Inequalities in Housing: An Examination of Recent Trends," *Demography* 19, 1 (1982): 37–51.

39. Karl E. Taeuber, "The Effect of Income Redistribution on Racial Residential Segregation," *Urban Affairs Quarterly* 4, 1 (1968): 5–14.

40. Karl E. Taeuber, "Negro Residential Segregation: Trends and Measurements," *Social Problems* 12, 1 (1964): 42–50.

41. Taeuber, "The Effect of Income Redistribution," 11.

42. Ibid., 12.

43. Pettigrew, "Racial Change and Social Policy," 123.

44. Ibid.

45. Ibid.

46. Ibid.

47. Brian I. Berry and John D. Kasarda, *Contemporary Urban Ecology* (New York: Macmillan, 1977); see also George C. Galster, *Black and White Preference for Segregation* (College of Wooster: Urban Studies Papers, September 1979).

48. Berry and Kasarda, *Contemporary Urban Ecology*; see also John F. Kain and John M. Quigley, *Housing Markets and Racial Discrimination: A Microeconomic Analysis* (New York: National Bureau of Economic Research, 1975).

49. Taeuber, "Negro Residential Segregation," 44.

50. Ibid.

51. Michael J. White, "The Measurement of Spatial Segregation," *American Journal of Sociology* 88, 5 (1983): 1008–1018; see also Thomas L. Van Valey, Wade Clark Roof, and Jerome E. Wilcox, "Trends in Residential Segregation 1960–1970," *American Journal of Sociology* 82, 4 (1977): 826–844.

52. White, "The Measurement of Spatial Segregation," 1008–1018.

53. Douglas S. Massey and Nancy A. Denton, "The Dimensions of Residential Segregation," *Social Forces* 67, 2 (1988): 281–315.

54. Stanley Lieberson, "An Asymmetrical Approach to Segregation," in *Ethnic Segregation in Cities*, eds. Ceri Peach, Vaughan Robinson, and Susan Smith (Athens: University of Georgia Press, 1981), 61–82.

55. Massey and Denton, "The Dimensions of Residential Segregation."

56. See, for example, Morton Deutsch and Mary Evans Collins, *Interracial Housing: A Psychological Evaluation of a Social Experiment* (Minneapolis: University of Minnesota Press, 1951).

57. David M. Gordon, "Capitalist Development and the History of American Cities," in *Marxism and the Metropolis: New Perspectives in Urban Political Economy*, ed. William K. Tabb and Larry Sawers, 2d ed. (New York: Oxford University Press, 1984), 55.

58. Ibid., 26–27.

59. Ibid. For a case study of Los Angeles County, see Charles Hoch, "City Limits: Municipal Boundary Formation and Class Segregation," in *Marxism and the Metropolis: New Perspectives in Urban Political Economy*, ed. William K. Tabb and Larry Sawers, 2d ed. (New York: Oxford University Press, 1984), 101–119.

60. Ibid., 33.

61. Ibid., 32.

62. Ibid.

63. Ibid., 44.

64. Ibid., 43.

65. "Because corporate headquarters were more unevenly distributed than nineteenth-century industrial establishments, many Industrial Cities, like Baltimore, St. Louis, and Cincinnati, never captured many of these headquarters." Ibid., 53.

66. Ibid., 54.

67. Ibid.

68. Harvey, *The Urbanization of Capital*, 123.

69. See, for example, Rodney D. Green, "Industrial Transition in the Land of Chattel Slavery: Richmond, Virginia, 1820–1860," *International Journal of Urban and Regional Research* 8, 2 (1984): 238–253; William R. Locklear, "The Celestials and the Angels: A Study of the Anti-Chinese Movement in Los Angeles to 1882," *Southern California Quarterly* 42 (1960): 239–256.

70. Robert C. Weaver, "Negro Labor since 1929," *Journal of Negro History* 35, 1 (1950): 21. In Chicago, according to the New York Times, "more than 70,000 Negro laborers . . . have agreed to accept a reduction in wages rather than lose their jobs." According to the President of the Unity Labor Union, "there were 100,000 unemployed Negroes in Chicago and vicinity." "70,000 Workers in Chicago Agree to Accept Wage Reductions Rather Than Lose Jobs," *New York Times* (12 December 1920): 14: 1.

3

Development of Low-Income Housing in the United States

Depressed economic and social conditions of the 1920s and early 1930s prompted the creation of low-income housing programs in the United States.

During the early period of subsidized housing (1932–1964), municipal authorities in developing corporate cities wanted to reverse the decline of their business districts; revitalize downtown areas; stimulate, for tax purposes, large-scale rebuilding; and halt the exodus of the middle class to the suburbs.[1] They often pursued these goals through programs of "slum clearance" and public housing construction. However, the financial resources needed for such programs were not available locally. If "urban renewal" was to proceed, federal intervention was needed.

By 1964, city renewal was no longer perceived to be contingent on the large-scale clearance of low-income areas and the relocation of their inhabitants. Instead, the challenging housing problem of established corporate cities was to stimulate the hard-to-rent sector of privately supplied housing and alleviate what was often called a vacancy crisis. In response to these new challenges, the methods and objectives of the federal housing program were modified to promote a "rational utilization of existing private units."

The provision of decent, safe, and sanitary housing for low- and moderate-income families remained, at best, an intermittent side-effect of these programs in both the early and the later periods of subsidized housing.

THE EARLY PERIOD, 1932–1964

The Problem and Early Response

Concrete federal involvement in low-income housing began under the Housing Division of the Public Works Administration (PWA), created by Title II of the National Industrial Recovery Act of 1933. This development came in the context of an intense debate about housing policies.[2]

Reactions to the idea of providing subsidized housing for low-income families varied greatly across the United States. Some cities, hard hit by the depression of the 1930s, earnestly requested federal grants for slum clearance and public housing. In 1936, New York City Mayor LaGuardia explained to the business community

We need low-income housing very badly in New York city. We need it as a matter of health precaution, as a matter of the morale of the people of our city, and in the long run it will pay. You will not see the returns immediately—the first or second or third year, but I assure you that the return to the taxpayer will be much greater than any loss in interest that might result from the elimination or even vacancy of existing . . . tenement houses.[3]

Other cities and states responded differently. Similar proposals for Pittsburgh and Baltimore were rejected by their mayors.[4] In Texas and California, federal housing programs were put to public referenda and often "voted out of town."[5]

Some have attributed this divergence of views to partisan differences, with politically liberal Democrats favoring public intervention on behalf of the poor more than conservative Republicans.[6] This explanation is at best incomplete, especially since little low-income housing materialized in most of the communities that participated in the federal housing program. But declining and depressed old industrial cities like New York and Chicago might be more interested in federally underwritten programs of clearance of low-income neighborhoods and public housing construction—with such immediate economic benefits as social relief and jobs for unemployed construction workers—than relatively new and expanding Western and Southwestern cities. It was also thought that in the long run, the decline of the central city could be directly reversed by the demolition of central-city low-income neighborhoods. In fact, we argue that this was the actual substantive goal of the program.[7]

A substantial need was partially revealed in a survey of real properties in sixty-four cities conducted by the Bureau of the Census in 1934. According to this survey, at the turn of the century much of the housing in the central areas of all major cities was already physically deteriorated, and some was unfit for human habitation.[8] This only worsened during the ensuing quarter-century, aggravated in the 1920s by overcrowding and a rapid decline of employment opportunities in many central cities. Census data show that between 1899 and 1929 the total central-city population of many major urban areas grew at a faster rate than the supply of gainful employment. The gap between the increase of the total population and the demand for labor was quite substantial in some areas, especially older Northeastern cities (see Table 3.1).[9]

Table 3.1
Total Population and Wage Earners in Selected Cities, 1899–1929

Cities & Outlying Areas	Percentage Increase of Population	Percentage Increase of Wage Earners	Relative Gap
New York	101.6	44.9	-56.7
New York Suburbs	204.3	136.1	-68.2
Chicago	98.8	83.3	-15.5
Chicago Suburbs	229.5	90.1	-139.4
Philadelphia	50.8	15.0	-35.8
Philadelphia Suburbs	104.3	77.5	-26.8
Detroit	449.1	472.1	23.0
Detroit Suburbs	411.7	364.1	-47.6
Los Angeles	1108.1	1369.6	261.5
L.A. Suburbs	1330.9	817.4	-513.5
Cleveland	135.9	165.4	29.5
Cleveland Suburbs	265.6	72.0	-193.6
St. Louis	42.9	68.1	25.2
St. Louis Suburbs	154.8	27.1	-127.7
Baltimore	58.1	28.7	-29.4
Baltimore Suburbs	37.3	-26.1	-63.4
Boston	39.3	37.2	-2.1
Boston Suburbs	74.6	-2.6	-77.2
Pittsburgh	48.3	-14.3	-62.6
Pittsburgh Suburbs	114.0	99.3	-14.7

Source: U.S. Department of Commerce, Bureau of the Census, *Location of Manufactures 1899–1929* (Washington, D.C.: U.S. Government Printing Office, 1933).

In New York City the total population more than doubled, while the supply of wage jobs increased by only 45 percent. Baltimore, Pittsburgh, Philadelphia, and Chicago had similar dynamic and growing gaps during that period.

In contrast, in many western cities (e.g., Los Angeles), the supply of wage jobs rose faster than the total population, as the movement of manufacturing from the Snowbelt to the Sunbelt began in earnest.[10]

A parallel disproportion in housing construction occurred. The total central-city population for cities of 100,000 or more grew between 1929 and 1937 despite the near cessation of new residential construction—new housing starts dropped by 90 percent between 1925 and 1930 to a mere 94,000 units a year.[11]

As industries expanded outward and the poverty population grew denser in the central city, business districts began to feel threatened by urban decay. Indeed, with the transformation of most cities from centers of manufacturing to centers of corporate headquarters, the withdrawal of factories and jobs from the central city created a complex problem of urban blight. In 1936, Wood found that the dwindling financial resources in many municipalities were diverted into activities such as law enforcement and social relief. In Indianapolis, for example, she estimated that "each person in the substandard area cost the taxpayer $28 as against $4 per person in other areas." Thirty percent of the city hospital service, more than 33 percent of public relief, and 36 percent of the city expenditure for arrests, trials, and imprisonment went into substandard areas that contained only 10 percent of the populations.[12] Similar patterns were evident in many other cities.[13]

It was in this context of economic depression and adjustment to the emerging corporate city that New Dealers and housing reformers urged Congress to supplement and stimulate the private housing sector by building low-cost housing for the "submerged middle-class." In 1937, Wood supported federal intervention in the housing market, arguing that a program of large scale clearance to provide shelter for low-income families could salvage "blighted areas" and make them "attractive and wholesome places" to live and invest.

In 1932, President Franklin Roosevelt approved the first legislation authorizing the Reconstruction Finance Corporation to make loans to limited-dividend corporations formed wholly for the purpose of providing housing for families of low income, or for the reconstruction of slum areas.[14] The actual activities of the agency, however, were limited to financing one project in New York.[15]

In 1933, the Housing Division of the Public Works Administration was created to replace the Reconstruction Finance Corporation and was empowered to undertake an experimental program of clearance and rehousing of families unable to afford decent housing in the private market. Initially the Housing Division was also intended to make loans and some grants to limited dividend corporations.[16] However, by 1934 only seven of approximately 500 applications had been approved by the Housing Division (see Table 3.2).[17]

Table 3.2
PWA Limited Dividend Projects,
1933–1934

Name of Limited Dividend Project	Location
Altavista Housing Corp.	Virginia
Boulevard Gardens Inc.	Queens, NY
Hillside Homes Corp.	Bronx, NY
Boylan Housing Corp.	Raleigh, NC
Carl Mackley Houses	Philadelphia, PA
Euclid Housing	Euclid, OH
Neighborhood Gardens	St. Louis, MO

Source: Housing Division, *Bulletin* 2 (August 1936).

Note: Does not include limited dividend projects financed by the RFC and private insurance companies.

This approach was soon discontinued. Federal studies indicated that the limited dividend corporations provided little finished housing and were slow to create jobs for unemployed workers in the building trades.[18] To remedy this situation, the Housing Division itself assumed the responsibility of acquiring and clearing sites and building housing projects under a formula which called for 55 percent of construction costs to be repaid from rent receipts with 3 percent annual interest for a period of sixty years.

This experimental PWA housing program was closely tied to the overall development of the corporate city. In nearly all of the thirty-six localities where it built public housing projects, the areas cleared were characterized more by their proximity to important business districts than by their prior industrial or low-income residential uses. In terms of preexisting housing of low-income families, the municipalities which participated in these PWA programs were not significantly worse off than those that did not—for example, Baltimore and Pittsburgh were nonparticipants.[19]

Between 1933 and 1937, the PWA built 21,640 units in forty-nine housing projects in thirty-six metropolitan areas. A total of 7,507 of these units were occupied by African-American tenants, over 60 percent of them in housing projects located in the South, even though the 1930 census reported only 8 percent of the urban population in this region of the country as African-American.

The high concentration of federally housed African-American tenants in the South did not necessarily imply that race relations in that region were in some sense *couleur de rose*, but instead probably represented attempts to stem the rapid migration of African-Americans to the North. The black proportions of the population of southern states had declined steadily as the result of interstate migration, from approximately 480 African-Americans for every 1,000 whites in the South in 1900 to 338 blacks for every 1,000, a 30 percent decrease, by 1930.[20] This phenomenon evoked the concerns described by a southern white woman in 1917:

That which a regard for common justice, fair play, human rights could not accomplish, a fear for our bank account is doing, and we are asking: Why is the Negro dissatisfied? What can we do to keep him in the South? We can't afford to let him go; he means too much for us—financially. He works for little; his upkeep costs us little, for we can house him in any kind of shack, and make him pay us well for that; we do not have to be careful of his living conditions; . . . and if he should happen to give us trouble we can cope with that and the law will uphold us in anything we do.[21]

So public housing already had a use contrary to its ostensible welfare character, in this case as a sort of social bribery to try to hold on to a class of cheap labor. As we shall see, this happened again on a much larger scale during World War II.

The USHA Program

In 1937, the United States Housing Act replaced the Housing Division of the PWA with the United States Housing Authority (USHA). The goal of the new housing authority was twofold; "to assist the several States and their subdivisions [in alleviating] present recurring unemployment, and [to] remedy the unsafe, and unsanitary housing conditions and the acute shortage of decent, safe and sanitary dwelling for families of low income in rural or urban communities."[22] Unlike the PWA, the new federal housing agency undertook no clearance or construction itself, since it was restricted to granting financial and technical aid to local Public Housing Authorities (PHAs).

The assistance to PHAs took two forms: loans covering up to 90 percent of the capital cost of developing housing projects and annual subsidies to help PHAs fill the funding gap between rent receipts and the operating and amortization costs of public housing projects.[23]

A special provision of the Housing Act, known as the "equivalent elimination," provided that for every unit destroyed by activities under this Act, a new public housing unit would have to be built.[24] This provision may have been the most important component of the legislation since it not only set the conditions under which a PHA could borrow funds for housing projects but also reassured private landlords that clearance for and construction of public housing would not interfere substantially in the private housing market. This provision reflected the limited scope for social change embodied in this program.

By decentralizing public housing programs, the Housing Act eliminated one objection directed against the experimental program of the Housing Division. Under the 1937 Housing Act, local authorities could decide for themselves how much public housing to construct. Indeed, this was logical since local governing bodies were now required to contribute financially to the development of public housing. In actual practice, local financial elites (e.g., bankers, savings and loan officials, insurance executives, and real estate brokers) selected sites to be cleared. Communities in which the development of the corporate city form was believed to be impeded by central-city slums were thus readily redeveloped, with the poor removed in the name of city reclamation. By contrast, those communities which felt no immediate threat to the corporate city form used local discretion to block or restrict the development of public housing even in the face of substantial shortages of housing for the poor. In Missouri, for example, the state legislature in 1939 restricted the creation of local housing authorities to the city of St. Louis. In California, proposed legislation to allow the creation of local housing authorities was vetoed by the governor in 1938.

In California, unlike older industrial states, the corporate city was built from scratch, not constructed on the bones of old neighborhoods. The public housing debate was therefore not framed in urgent economic and political terms as in the Northeast. In 1938 the Director of the Los Angeles Municipal Housing Commission complained to no avail:

Just what can be done in California now is a matter of the greatest uncertainty. Our efforts to educate the people of the state must be redoubled. A campaign to expose the present living conditions of our lower income groups must be planned and carried out. The present low-rent housing shortage must be fully publicized. The existing rental situation must be made clear and the absurd charges for unsafe, insanitary, and overcrowded housing accommodations must be made known. The outrageous mortgage structure must be brought out into the open. And finally, the land speculation evil with its chaotic system of land valuation utterly divorced from use valuation, must be rigorously exposed. This, of course, is no small task, and the necessary financial support for such a campaign is not easily found. Local selfish interest will fight, tooth and claw to preserve the status quo. Our consolation is that other groups in other municipalities have done it and we should therefore be able to do it too.[25]

It was not until World War II and the war housing programs that public housing in California and several other western states became an accepted reality.

Racially, clearance activities affected African-Americans more adversely than whites. The Housing Authority of St. Petersburg, Florida, in its 1938 application for a loan from the USHA, bluntly described a proposed clearance and public housing project:

We propose to clear an area known as Methodist Town (colored) which is located on the north side of town within two blocks of the second most important business intersection. We propose to locate the low-cost housing in an area which is conceded to the Negroes on the south side of town, *approximately two miles from the center* [emphasis added]. This requires the purchase of two sites and the use of only one. We believe we can guarantee the return of the investment in the site of the slum-clearance project to the low-cost housing project. If given a sufficient amount of time, say five years, from the date of acquisition of title of the slum-clearance site, we can resell the property, taking advantage of the anticipated increase in valuation, for an amount which will refund the entire cost of acquiring the site and clearance. We have asked the USHA to underwrite this amount for a period of five years, the request being made after we were informed that a direct grant for this part of our project would not be made. As a result of the recent refunding of the city's obligation and indebtedness, we unfortunately had no collateral to offer as security to guarantee a loan from the USHA for this part of the project, but we are hoping for a favorable decision.[26]

The War Housing Program

In 1941, four years after its inauguration, the program of public housing of the United States Housing Authority was suspended as the president, by Executive Order, reorganized all federal housing agencies into a single National Housing Administration with the mission of consolidating and subordinating the production of public housing to the needs of the war.[27] The Lanham Act subsequently mandated the transfer of public (and some private) housing units to the War and Navy Departments.[28] In 1942, the Federal Public Housing Authority (FPHA) was established to replace the USHA.

The new agency was not involved in urban renewal.[29] Its primary mission was to attract workers to war production and keep them on their jobs by offering them special housing incentives through three emergency programs.[30] These were the Public War Housing Program, consisting of permanent and temporary housing built under the Lanham Act; the Homes Conversion Program, authorizing the federal government to lease private housing accommodations and convert them into temporary housing for war workers; and the Veterans' Reuse Housing Program, created to alleviate the housing shortage of returning war veterans by offering temporary housing for their use.

Most of these programs were not permanent. The intention of the FPHA was to divest itself of all interest in the properties involved and turn them over to the private market.[31] Section 4 of the Lanham Act, apparently inserted after intense lobbying by landlord associations, stipulated that it was

the policy to further the national defense by providing housing in those areas where it cannot otherwise be provided by private enterprise when needed, and that such housing may be sold and disposed of as expeditiously as possible: Provided, that in disposing of said housing consideration shall be given to its full market value and said housing or any part thereof shall not, unless specifically authorized by Congress, be conveyed to any public or private agency organized for slum clearance or to provide subsidized housing for persons of low income.[32]

The war housing program was short lived but financially and organizationally more vibrant than its predecessors, the PWA and USHA. In three years, from 1941 to 1943, the total supply of defense-related housing quadrupled from 331,567 units to 1,339,254 units; the publicly financed component accounted for about half of the stock throughout.

Postwar Public Housing

Following World War II, the future of public housing was uncertain. For some years no new construction of subsidized housing was authorized by Congress except for veteran reuse housing (a housing program for returning World War II veterans). Meanwhile, the administration of existing housing was increasingly dominated by real estate and banking executives. In 1946 about 45 percent of commissioners of local housing authorities were bankers, businessmen, or industrialists. "A breakdown of the banker–businessman–industrialist classification, which includes real estate and saving and loan officials, insurance brokers, and bankers, shows that bankers lead the group with 356 commissioners. Within the banking group are 100 banking executives and 153 real estate and saving and loan officials. In the professional group lawyers lead with 124 commissioners; physicians and dentists number 49 . . . and welfare workers 12."[33] The role of public housing agencies during this period was to "dispose of" war housing, remove "income ineligible" families, and "restore the program to its designated purpose."[34] In particular, housing projects originally built by the PWA[35] and the USHA, as wellas projects built during the war with funds transferred from the USHA to the War and Navy Departments, were returned to "civilian" use.[36]

In 1949, 193,807 units of public housing were available for occupancy. Over half of these units were located in the North, and nearly 70 percent of these (over one-third of the total) were in five industrial states (New York, New Jersey, Illinois, Pennsylvania, and Ohio) where economic pressures for urban reorganization were most acute.[37]

Urban Renewal and Public Housing

In 1949, the United States enacted an amendment to the Housing Act of 1937, which stated as a national policy that "every American family [was] entitled to a decent home in a proper living environment."[38] The new law authorized the Public Housing Administration to complete 810,000 units of public housing in increments of 135,000 units a year from 1949 through 1955.[39]

Unlike previous housing programs, public housing under the 1949 law was explicitly defined as an instrument of urban renewal.[40] According to the National Commission on Urban Problems the government wanted to "help cities to collect more taxes" through urban renewal by bringing back the middle class and making a "better use of downtown land, stimulate private investment, and restore civic pride."[41] Families displaced by urban renewal activities were to be rehoused in "decent safe and sanitary dwellings . . . available at rents and prices within their means."[42] However, no assistance would be given to displaced single individuals or families with incomes above the admission limit for public housing. And despite the provision to rehouse displaced low-income families, low-income areas in many cities were cleared without replacement housing for displaced families ever being built, suggesting that the primary intent of the program was not social welfare.[43] Indeed, the production goals established in 1949 were not reached.[44] Instead, from 1952 to 1954, the program constructed 50,000, 35,000, and 20,000 units respectively, and thereafter, produced between 35,000 and 45,000 units per year. As of 1961, only 321,405 of the 810,000 units initially projected for 1955 had actually been completed, or even contracted.[45] A disappointed Senator Paul Douglas, often called the "champion of housing for the poor," recalled that "We authorized 135,000 units a year for six years, which would have meant if that had been carried out we would have had 810,000 units in 1955. . . . Now we find ourselves, 16 years after this Act was passed, with 581,000 units actually in operation, including some, I am sure, of the war period."[46]

Barely half of families and individuals displaced by urban renewal activities ever received federal relocation payments. The National Commission on Urban Problems estimated that these payments averaged less than $80 per family through 1967;[47] the 1967–1968 average payment rose slightly but at less than $90, remained significantly below the maximum of $200 per family established in 1959.

Although the Housing Act of 1949 added significant numbers of units to the public housing stock, it served, and was primarily designed, to help the reorganization of central-city business districts. Low-income families and individuals were displaced from their neighborhoods not to be rehoused into "decent safe and sanitary" dwellings, as the housing act ostensibly called for, but to free the land they had occupied for new investment. In 1968, the National Advisory Commission on Civil Disorders estimated that during the 1950s, only 4 million out of 16.8 million new housing units constructed throughout the country were built in central cities. During the same period, over 1.5 million central-city units were lost through demolition and other means. Despite a decline of substandard units nationwide, the number of minority (mainly African-American) families living in substandard housing increased from 1.4 to 1.8 million between 1950 and 1960.[48] For supporters of public housing this "dreary deadlock" was disappointing. Said Robert Weaver, "to those like myself who have fought for and worked for public housing, this is disheartening. But more importantly, it is a dangerous trend which must be recognized by the American people. It is also unnecessary and uncalled for, since it could have been . . . avoided."[49]

THE MODERN PERIOD, 1964–1992

Early federal housing programs facilitated the relocation of low-income families and individuals from areas in or near business districts and thus contributed to the redevelopment of the central city. Turning to the economic context of the evolution of low-income housing policies from the 1960s through the 1980s, we find that, in contrast, the modern period of low-income housing in the United States has been generally characterized: (1) by an expanding web of civil rights laws that narrowly prohibit racial segregation and discrimination in government housing programs; (2) by the completion of the transition to the corporate form of urban settlement; and (3) by a decline in the use of large-scale clearance and relocation for central-city reorganization. A new method of subsidizing housing, namely direct rent supplements to eligible low-income families which would allow them to seek better housing in the private market than they would be able to afford on their own, attracted wide interest in the early 1960s. For many municipalities, the preservation of the private housing market, particularly the segment occupied by the poor, was becoming politically and economically important and thus requiring direct attention.

To address the vacancy crisis, the federal government expanded its housing subsidy programs to include the support of privately owned housing units. According to one description of this new approach to low-income housing, "If poor households were given additional purchasing power, and if they chose to spend substantial proportions of that purchasing power on housing, then they could effectively demand housing of higher quality. Additionally, since program recipients would be renting existing units, rather than living in new housing specially built as subsidized housing, lower program costs were anticipated. [These] demand-augmenting voucher programs are called *housing allowances*."[50]

These allowances were seen to have at least three advantages over traditional public housing. First, because "the cost of slum-clearance and new construction was higher than the lease of existing units," a given amount of federal subsidies would serve more low-income families if used for housing allowances than if spent on clearance and new construction.[51] Second, housing allowances would allow more "freedom of choice" among residential neighborhoods for low-income families.[52] Robert Embry, then commissioner of housing and community development for the city of Baltimore, testified at a 1970 Senate hearing that, "A proposal to provide rent subsidies in private housing . . . is extremely desirable. It fosters full utilization of existing properties, it does not encourage concentration of low income families, and it avoids the many barriers to racial integration that have effectively thwarted such efforts. . . . I am convinced that this approach is the only valid program to house low income families . . . that can achieve a dramatic and significant impact."[53] The third perceived advantage was that housing allowances would curb the corruption and inefficiency allegedly inherent in government owned and operated housing by relying on a putatively more efficient private housing market.

Setting aside, for a moment, the individual merits of the alternative methods of delivering housing to the poor, a fundamental question remains: Why were housing allowance programs implemented in the 1960s but not in the 1930s? Indeed, proposals for demand-augmenting vouchers (housing allowances) are actually as old as federal housing assistance.[54] Debates on the relative merits of demand and supply-oriented housing programs were no more sophisticated in the 1960s than previously. Moreover, the shift from primarily clearance and new construction to allowances also cannot be attributed to empirical evidence of relative effectiveness, since such evidence (e.g., from the 1973 Experimental Housing Allowance Program) became available only long after the voucher subsidy approach had been implemented. The shift is in fact another indication that federal housing programs have not fundamentally been about housing.

Leased Housing and Turnkey

The 1965 Housing and Urban Development Act amended the Housing Act of 1937, introducing Section 23 (revised somewhat in 1970) which authorized local housing authorities to lease privately owned housing and, in effect, sublet it to housing authority tenants. In other words, the public housing supervised by a public housing authority could now include units the PHA leased from private owners as well as units it owned itself.[55] This prototype housing allowance program was intended to be a cheap and rapid method of expanding the supply of low-rent housing for families who could not afford private market housing. It allowed local housing authorities to lease units from private owners for use as public housing. Eligible low-income families were also allowed to make choices from units offered by private owners under the "finder-keeper" provision.

The authors of Section 23 strove to create the impression that low-income families could have real freedom of choice in the private housing market. Nevertheless, a 1975 review of the leased housing program by the General Accounting Office confirmed what many observers had suspected: Section 23 had proven to be a poor source of housing for low-income families. This was also the case for other variations of the housing allowance paradigm of the era, partly because the supplement rarely brought actual rents in privately owned housing within the reach of eligible families.[56]

The Section 8 Housing Assistance Program

The Section 8 Housing Assistance Program, currently the largest source of subsidized low-income housing in the country, was authorized in 1974 following the FHA default crisis. It provides housing assistance payments by the federal government on behalf of eligible low- and moderate-income families through four different subprograms: New Construction, Substantial Rehabilitation, Moderate Rehabilitation, and Existing. New Construction is largely used by private developers who obtain financing and build low-income housing projects. The subsidy is in the form of payments on behalf of the eligible tenants which effectively lower the rent to 30 percent of the eligible family's adjusted annual income. Substantial Rehabilitation, Moderate Rehabilitation, and Existing operate similarly, covering already constructed, privately owned buildings needing various degrees of rehabilitation or none. This is also a "finder-keeper" provision.[57]

Unfortunately, Section 8 assistance has also fallen short of demand as the National Association of Housing and Redevelopment Officials indicated in 1986. A survey of waiting lists in 223 local housing authorities by the Association revealed that 782,000 families were on waiting lists for public housing, with an overall average wait of more than one year. Average waits were much higher in some places: five years in the Winston–Salem MSA and seven years in Atlantic City.[58] Some were not even allowed to wait. The survey revealed that waiting lists had been closed in some PHAs, including eight of the fourteen largest, because the number of applicants far exceeded the projected supply of units.

SUMMARY

The history of low-income housing in the United States indicates that federal housing programs, which grew out of the Depression of 1929, soon became an instrument of central-city reorganization and renewal. Until the 1960s, the primary role of low-income housing in most cities was to facilitate the removal of the poor from areas inside or adjacent to business districts, thus advancing the transition of older industrial cities to corporate cities. The formal adoption of public housing did not necessarily mean that housing conditions of the poor and displaced were significantly improved. Between 1934 and 1938 over one million individuals were displaced from central-city areas as a result of clearance activities nationwide.[59] Only a small fraction of these displaced people could have received federal housing assistance, since as of 1938 fewer than 22,000 units were completed and available for occupancy and only about 65,000 additional units had been authorized (on some of which construction had not even began).[60]

In terms of its impact on the housing conditions of the poor, the 22,000 units of low-income housing could have little effect on the nearly one-third of the population described as ill housed. Between 1941 and 1945, the supply of subsidized housing units grew more rapidly because of wartime exigencies. Many of these units were liquidated or demolished in the immediate post-war period, thus removing them from the stock of subsidized housing units.

During the early phases of urban renewal and redevelopment (1950–1962), clearance and relocation activities accelerated. Despite the rapid increase in the number of displaced families and individuals, however, the majority of those eligible for housing assistance were not rehoused by the federal program.

During the modern period of low-income housing, the physical reorganization of the central city had generally been achieved. Low-income residents of areas inside the business districts and nearby areas had in large part been relocated elsewhere in the city. The challenge of the era that needed to be met with the help of the federal housing program was how to expand and rationally utilize the segment of the private housing market serving low-income people. New housing programs, each heavily dependent on private landlords and developers (both previously considered the principal culprits in the housing impasse of the poor) were successively introduced. Although the redesigned programs were expected to increase the supply of housing for the poor in nonimpacted areas at a lower cost to the government, no more than 7 percent of the eligible population received housing assistance.

NOTES

1. National Commission on Urban Problems, *Building the American City: Report of the Natoinal Commission on Urban Problems* (New York: Praeger, 1969), 88; see also Herbert J. Gans, "Human Implications of Current Redevelopment and Relocation Planning," *Journal of the American Institute of Planners* (February 1959): 15–25.

2. For an earlier example of this debate, see Jacob August Riis, *The Battle with the Slums* (New York: Macmillan, 1902). See also Jacob August Riis, *How the Other Half Lives: Studies among the Tenements of New York* (New York: Sagamore Press, 1957).

3. "New York Mayor, Business Men Demand Public Housing," *Public Housing Progress* (10 June 1936): 2.

4. Letter addressed to the National Public Housing Conference from William N. McNair, Mayor, City of Pittsburgh, who wrote: "It is no function of government to provide people with houses. Nor is it a function of government to finance housing. . . . It is primarily the Federal octopus that is responsible for our general poverty. . . . This public housing service is just one more extension of government exactions of all of us and making most of us poor—too poor to build our own homes. . . . While ostensibly engaged in abolishing old slums—you are actually producing new ones. The PWA should be abolished forthwith." *Public Housing Progress* 1, 3 (1935): 3.

5. Lawrence M. Friedman, "Public Housing and the Poor: An Overview," *California Law Review* 54 (1966): 645. For a list of states and municipalities that accepted the public housing program, see "Project Roll Call: A Review of Large-Scale Rental Housing Projects," *Housing Yearbook* (1938): 118–133; "State and Local Activity," *Housing Yearbook* (1939): 1–102; Catherine Bauer, "The First Six Months of USHA,"

Housing Yearbook (1938): 1–9; Elizabeth Longan, "Progress by Local and State Agencies," *Housing Yearbook* (1938): 40–117.

6. See, for example, Peter Marcuse, "The Beginnings of Public Housing in New York," *Journal of Urban History* 12, 4 (1986): 353–390.

7. General concerns about the housing conditions of the poor, though longstanding, had previously been insufficient to elicit federal intervention in the private housing market. What made the program of the PWA possible in the early 1930s was the manifest need to smooth the transition of declining industrial cities to the corporate city structures, not the bad housing conditions of the poor. Before the PWA, during World War I, the federal government was involved in the housing market. The primary objective of the involvement was to entice war workers to stay on their jobs. The government, through the U.S. Housing Corporation (USHC), built nearly 100 projects for 21,000 families of workers engaged in the war production at a total cost of over $100,000,000. The enabling legislation called an "Act to authorize the President to provide housing for war needs" was passed by Congress in May 1918. It gave the president (after an amendment in June 1918) the authority to use the $100,000,000 provided by Section 8 of the Act to build housing, transportation, and other facilities related to the living and working conditions of war workers. The primary goal of USHC was to "increase the efficiency of labor" by reducing its turnover rates and housing-related labor discontents. The "Ten-Day Committee" appointed to investigate the housing of workers employed on government contracts urged that the lack of housing facilities was sufficiently extensive to "menace the quick production of ships and war materials" and that the relation of housing to the war program was direct. U.S. Department of Labor, Bureau of Industrial Housing and Transportation, *War Emergency Construction: Report of the U.S. Housing Corporation*, no. 1 (Washington, D.C.: U.S. Government Printing Office, 1919); see also Electus D. Litchfield, "Yorkship Village in 1917 and 1939," *The American City* 54, 11 (1939): 42–43.

8. According to N. H. Engle of the Bureau of Foreign and Domestic Commerce, "in 64 cities more than 600,000 homes had neither bathtub nor shower, and nearly 450,000 were without indoor water closets. These figures comprise 23 and 17 percent, respectively, of all residential units surveyed," *Public Housing Progress* 1 (1934): 1.

9. U.S. Department of Commerce, Bureau of the Census, *Location of Manufactures 1899–1929: A Study of the Tendencies toward Concentration and toward Dispersion of Manufactures in the United States* (Washington D.C.: U.S. Government Printing Office, 1933): 36; see also U.S. Department of Commerce, Bureau of the Census, *Changes in Distribution of Manufacturing Wage Earners 1899–1939* (Washington, D.C.: U.S. Government Printing Office, 1933).

10. Ibid., 66–67.

11. William Ebenstein, "The Law of Public Housing," *Minnesota Law Review* 23, 7 (1939): 879–924.

12. Edith Elmer Wood, "The Costs of Bad Housing," *The Annals of the American Academy of Political and Social Sciences* 190 (1937); see also Coleman Woodbury, *Costs of Slums and Blighted Areas* (Chicago: National Association of Housing Officials, Bulletin 99).

13. Ebenstein, "The Law of Public Housing," 883.

14. The Reconstruction Finance Corporation was organized to "make loans to corporations formed wholly for the purpose of providing housing for families of low income, or for the reconstruction of slum areas, which are regulated by state or mu-

nicipal law as to rents, charges, capital structure, rate of returns, and areas and methods of operation. . . ." Public Law 302, 72d Cong., 1st sess. (1932).

15. One additional limited dividend housing project was financed by the RFC. The project was the Wilroads Gardens in Dodge City, Kansas. National Housing Conference, *Public Housing Tour Guide* (New York: 1 December 1940): 46.

16. The method of financing limited dividend housing projects was adopted in the George-Healey Act of 1935. Prior to this act, federal grants were limited to 30 percent of the cost of proposed housing projects. The remaining 70 percent were loans at 4 percent interest. "Public Housing," *The Architectural Forum* (May 1938): 345–349.

17. "Urban Housing: The Story of PWA Housing Division 1933–1936," *Bulletin* 2 (August 1936).

18. In 1935, $450,000,000 was granted for housing, of which $221,982,000 was allotted to the PWA Housing Division. Since the main purpose of the new legislation was to provide the greatest number of jobs in the shortest time possible, examination of the work of the PWA was made. Results showed that housing did not create employment for as many persons as did some other types of projects. In view of that fact the president rescinded $120,608,950 in 1935. Gilbert A. Cam, "United States Government Activity in Low-Cost Housing, 1932–1938," *Journal of Political Economy* (June 1938): 363.

19. See Public Housing Administration, Records of the Housing Division of PWA, 1933–1937, RG196, "Application of Capitol Planning and Housing Corporation, Atlanta, Georgia, November 23, 1933," National Archives.

20. See U.S. Department of Commerce, Bureau of the Census, *Negroes in the United States 1920–1932* (Washington, D.C.: U.S. Government Printing Office, 1935), 13.

21. W. E. B. Du Bois, "The Migration of Negroes," *The Crisis* (June 1917): 63–66.

22. Housing and Home Finance Agency, Public Housing Administration, *Federal Laws, Low-Rent Public Housing, the United States Housing Act of 1937 and Related Laws as Amended through October 15, 1964* (Washington, D.C.: Housing and Home Finance Agency, 1964), 1; see also Public Law 412, 75th Cong., 1st sess. (September 1937).

23. The United States Housing Act also required local contributions to the operation of housing projects in the form either of tax exemption to housing projects or a commitment to provide adequate municipal services to tenants without additional charge.

24. Federal Works Agency, United States Housing Authority, "Equivalent Elimination of Unsafe or Insanitary Dwellings," *Bulletin No. 3 on Policy and Procedure* (15 April 1940); see also "When the USHA Buys Land," *The New Republic* (25 October 1939): 341–343.

25. Federal Works Agency, United States Housing Authority, "Equivalent Elimination of Unsafe or Insanitary Dwellings," 43.

26. Longan, "Progress by Local and State Agencies," 53.

27. John B. Blandford, Jr., "The National Housing Agency," *Housing Yearbook* (1944): 21–26; see also "The Reorganization of Federal Housing Agencies," *Housing Yearbook* (1942): 1–9.

28. "By the end of 1941, the public housing was on a 100 percent war footing." Herbert Emmerich, "Public Housing in 1941," *Housing Yearbook* (1942): 10; "The Reorganization of Federal Housing Agencies," 1–9; Public Law 671, 76th Cong. (June

1940); Public Law 849, 76th Cong. (October 1940); Nathan Strauss, "Public Housing 1940–1941: A Review of the United States Housing Authority's Activities," *Housing Yearbook* (1941): 226–239.

29. During the war, slum-clearance projects—known as PL 671 projects—were built with funds transferred from the USHA or transferred from the PWA and USHA programs to the War and Navy Department. PL 671 housing projects were intended to be returned to local housing authorities after the war. Therefore, despite the construction during the war of a limited number of slum-clearance projects by the FPHA, the agency was never concerned with urban renewal and urban beautification.

30. Although the program of the FPHA was described as "subsidized" housing, tenants were effectively paying what these structures were worth. In 1943, for example, rents in 98 percent of war housing projects "varied only from an average of $31.65 per month for the lowest income group to $33.99 for the highest, a narrow range which [reflected] FPHA's policy to build dwellings of a more or less uniform character and to set rents based on the market. . . . [The tenants] were probably paying a smaller proportion of income for rent than they would [have] if they were selecting from an unlimited market, they [were] paying what the FPHA housing accommodations [were] worth." "FPHA Rents," *FPHA Bulletin* 52 (September 1943): 3.

31. The Mutual Ownership concept of the Lanham Act was one of the mechanisms used to liquidate permanent defense housing projects in the private market. Under this option of the Lanham Act, a nonprofit corporation of tenants took title of entire housing projects and "sold a right of perpetual occupancy to each resident for an amount equal to his pro rata share of the entire purchase price." Emmerich, "Public Housing in 1943," 40–41; see also U.S. Housing and Home Finance Agency, *Annual Report* (Washington, D.C.: U.S. Housing and Home Finance Agency, 1950), 393.

32. Federal Works Agency, Office of the General Counsel, *Lanham Act As Amended to July 15, 1943*, prepared by Minnie Wiener, Librarian Law Library (Washington, D.C.: July 1943).

33. "Majority of LHA Members Are Bankers, Businessmen or Industrialists," *FPHA Bulletin* 4, 2 (1947): 2–3.

34. U.S. Housing and Home Finance Agency, *Annual Report* (1950): 337.

35. Ibid., 335.

36. "Majority of LHA Members Are Bankers, Businessmen or Industrialists," 2–3.

37. Robert C. Weaver, "Poverty in America: The Role of Urban Renewal," in *Poverty in America: Proceedings of a National Conference Held at the University of California at Berkeley, 26–28 February 1965*, ed. Margaret S. Gordon (San Francisco: Chandler, 1965), 326.

38. U.S. Housing and Home Finance Agency, *Annual Report* (1950): 322.

39. Ibid., 323–324.

40. U.S. Housing and Home Finance Agency, *Annual Report* (1952).

41. National Commission on Urban Problems, *Building the American City,* 88.

42. Raymond N. Foley, John Taylor Egan, and Nathaniel S. Keith, *Statement on the Relationship of the Slum-Clearance and Low-Rent Housing Programs* (Washington, D.C.: U.S. Housing and Home Finance Agency, 1950): 1.

43. Robert C. Weaver, *Habitation with Segregation: Address before the National Committee against Discrimination in Housing* (New York: National Committee Against Discrimination in Housing, 1952), 75.

44. U.S. Housing and Home Finance Agency, *Annual Report.*

45. U.S. Department of Housing and Urban Development, *Statistical Yearbook* (Washington, D.C.: U.S. Government Printing Office, 1976), 158.

46. National Housing Conference, *The Housing Yearbook* (Washington, D.C.: U.S. Government Printing Office, 1965), 4.

47. National Commission on Urban Problems, *Building the American City*, 80–91.

48. Some observers have described urban renewal in the United States as a racist program operated to the detriment of the minority population in favor of businesses and central-city governments. In essence, this criticism has been limited to objections to the small federal relocation payments made to displaced low-income persons rather than to the policy of displacing the poor to make downtown areas attractive to business investment. For example, Richard Bingham suggested that to "remove the racist overtones from urban renewal, several changes are necessary. First, Congress, HUD, and the general public must recognize the program for what it is—a program oriented (through its application) to downtown and near downtown redevelopment. There is no sin in utilizing urban renewal for this purpose, the sin is not recognizing that this is the way the program is being operated. Without urban renewal programs, or some similar form of federal aid, there would be very little downtown redevelopment in U.S. cities. It is only in the 'boom' cities such as Austin that private enterprise can afford to undertake downtown redevelopment projects on its own. Once the true purpose of urban renewal is recognized, it is then necessary to change the program so that it is no longer racist in nature. This can be done by converting renewal to a nonzero-sum game so that everyone will benefit from the renewal process. As it stands now, the city and the business community are the winners in the renewal process while the black community and other minorities lose (an admitted oversimplification). If the black and minority communities were also winners in the renewal process, urban renewal would no longer operate as a zero-sum game and the program would no longer be racist in nature." Richard D. Bingham, *Public Housing and Urban Renewal: An Analysis of Federal–Local Relations* (New York: Praeger, 1975), 227.

49. Weaver, *Habitation with Segregation*, 75.

50. Raymond J. Struyk and Marc Bendick, Jr., eds., *Housing Vouchers for the Poor: Lessons from a National Experiment* (Washington, D.C.: Urban Institute Press, 1981), 5.

51. "It is at least twice as expensive to build new units to house low-income households as it is to assist poor households to rent existing units. Although the justification for new construction programs has often been the goal of shoring up the building industry, the available evidence suggests that most subsidized new construction displaces private building activity, and that government programs tend to increase rather than to reduce instability in the new industry." John F. Kain, "America's Persistent Housing Crises: Errors in Analysis and Policy," *The Annals of the American Academy of Political and Social Science* 465 (1983): 147.

52. Struyk and Bendick, *Housing Vouchers*, 31.

53. Ibid., 30.

54. See, for example, "When the USHA Buys Land," *The New Republic* (25 October 1939): 341–343; see also Struyk and Bendick, *Housing Vouchers*, 33–40.

55. In 1956 and 1959, the public housing program was expanded to include the construction of units under two new housing programs. The first of these programs, (initially authorized in 1956) was known as Elderly Housing and was designed to provide low-cost housing accommodations for senior citizens. The second (initially

authorized in 1959) was known as the Section 202 loan program and was designed to provide "independent living" for elderly and handicapped persons by authorizing direct federal loans to nonprofit sponsors of low-rent housing for elderly or handicapped persons. Unlike public housing, housing projects under the Section 202 are owned and operated by their sponsors.

56. To the question "Would landlords rehabilitate substandard properties and increase maintenance?" researchers at the Urban Institute monitoring the EHAP program concluded that "the more stringent the program standards and hence the greater the amount of repairs needed to pass the standard on average, the less likely improvements were to take place . . . renters qualify more often by moving than homeowners do." Struyk and Bendick, *Housing Vouchers*, 14.

57. U.S. Department of Housing and Urban Development, Office of Policy Development and Research, *Public Housing Agency Administrative Practices: Handbook for the Section 8 Existing Housing Program* (Washington, D.C.: U.S. Government Printing Office, 1979), 11; see also U.S. Department of Housing and Urban Development, Office of Policy Development and Research, *Housing in the Seventies: A Report of the National Housing Policy Review* (Washington, D.C.: U.S. Department of Housing and Urban Development, 1974).

58. National Association of Housing and Redevelopment Officials (NAHRO), *This Is Public Housing* (Washington, D.C.: National Association of Housing and Redevelopment Officials, 1988).

59. Compared to the estimated need of 5.6 million units to provide minimally decent housing for Americans, this effort was still far below the social need. According to the *Architectural Forum*, "If the need for a coherent policy is measured by the size of the problem it attacks, there is no greater need in this country today than for a policy on subsidies for housing. In its report to the Senate on the Housing Bill, the Committee on Education and Labor gave two measurements of the size of the problem—which is, of course, also the size of the group now poorly housed. The irreducible minimum as represented by 'existing dwellings absolutely unfit for further habitation, which should be condemned and demolished immediately' was 5,663,000 units." "Subsidies for Housing," *Architectural Forum* (April 1938): 309.

60. The Public Housing Progress reported in 1938 that the New York City housing authority received more than 14,000 applications for a 574-unit Harlem River House. Peter Marcuse reported a number that was 1,000 higher. Peter Marcuse, "The Beginnings of Public Housing," 375.

4

Research Procedure

METHODOLOGY

Segregation in subsidized housing is most visible in the patterns of racial occupancy within and among projects, and historically only this racially based form of segregation has been studied.[1] This limited approach changed in 1974 when Congress recognized, in the Housing and Community Development Act, the exclusive placement of low-rent housing projects in low-income areas as an important aspect of segregation. Elizabeth Warren, for example, noted that

One of the major issues of the 1960s' Civil Rights movement was the concentration of low-income public housing in inner-city areas and the segregation of the projects by race. Policies began to change in the 1960s and 1970s, however, as a result of landmark efforts. . . . The thrust was *toward dispersing low-income subsidized housing to white city and suburban neighborhoods to bring about racial integration. In addition, dispersal was directed toward middle- and upper-income neighborhoods to reduce the segregation by income as well as by race.* It was thought that low-income people generally, whites as well as blacks, would benefit from dispersal [emphasis added].[2]

Nevertheless, few studies have clearly analyzed placement of subsidized housing projects specifically in terms of income factors.

The most cursory review of subsidized housing in the United States reveals that housing projects tend to be clustered in low-income areas and predominantly occupied by tenants from one racial group. It is useful to distinguish these two concepts. Formally, *racial segregation* in subsidized housing is defined to be the separation of tenants by race in individual housing projects or buildings. The higher the relative concentration of tenants from the same racial group in an individual housing project, the greater is the degree of racial segregation; the lower the concentration, the smaller is the degree of racial segregation.[3] *Income separation* in subsidized housing is defined to be the relative concentration of housing projects in one income area (defined mathematically below) regardless of racial occupancy. The greater the physical concentration of housing projects in one income area, the greater the degree of income separation; the more uniform such distribution, the smaller the degree of income separation.

Operationally, a Public Housing Authority (PHA) can be divided into discrete income areas based on economic criteria. Ideally, an income area should be economically homogeneous with the distribution of the annual household income highly concentrated around its mean and with little variation in the quality of social amenities available to residents. Moreover, income areas should be qualitatively different from one another, although the social amenities available in different residential neighborhoods are difficult to summarize quantitatively. Nevertheless, by using the median household income in different residential tracts as the indicator of income area, any metropolitan area or PHA jurisdiction can be divided at a simple level into discrete areas. (Note that this definition of income area implies that spatially discontinuous residential tracts can belong to the same income area. Indeed, an income area will be spatially continuous only if all residential tracts with median household income not exceeding the predefined threshold are spatially contiguous, presumably an unlikely occurrence. However, we will in fact use entire municipalities as proxies for income areas, as will be described.)

For this study, each PHA is bifurcated into the low-income area and the moderate-high-income area, which are defined later in this chapter in ad hoc fashion based on the nonavailability of data. It is important to note that income separation and racial segregation are, in principle, independent and can combine in any fashion in particular cases, as illustrated in Table 4.1. Here, *A* represents the case of tenants both racially and economically separated. The tenants represented by *B* are not separated by race but are separated by income. Housing projects are evenly distributed among existing income areas, but tenants are racially segregated in scenario *C*. Finally, *D* depicts housing projects that are evenly distributed among income areas and racially neutral in occupancy—no segregation exists. Table 4.1 illustrates the combinations of factors that become apparent when segregation in low-income housing is defined as a two-dimensional phenomenon.

Table 4.1
Relations between Racial Occupancy and Income
Dispersal of Projects

	Patterns of Racial Occupancy	
Patterns of Income Dispersal	Racially Homogeneous	Racially Neutral
Concentrated in One Income Area	A	B
Dispersed among All Income Areas	C	D

To be integrated in both senses, therefore, a subsidized low-rent housing program must contain units that are racially neutral in occupancy and housing projects that are evenly dispersed among income areas.[4]

Measuring Income Dispersal in Principle

The distribution of subsidized low-rent housing projects among income areas in a PHA has rarely been studied statistically. Spacial segregation of racial groups in urban areas, however, has been measured by the index D of residential dissimilarity and its variations. This procedure will be adapted to measure income separation in this study.

The index D of residential dissimilarity of whites and blacks is expressed

$$D = \frac{1}{2} \sum_{i}^{N} |\, w_{1i} - w_{2i} \,| * 100 \qquad (2)$$

where w_{1i} is the proportion of the white population that resides in tract i, w_{2i} is the proportion of the black population that resides in tract i, and N is the number of tracts in the city (see Equation [1] in Chapter 2 and the discussion there).[5]

The same principles can be adapted to measure income separation using the following logic. If all income areas in a given PHA's territory have the same proportions of subsidized and nonsubsidized (private) housing, then the distribution of subsidized and nonsubsidized housing among income areas is even (i.e., fully integrated). If, on the other hand, some income areas have significantly higher proportions of the jurisdiction's subsidized housing, and others have significantly lower shares of subsidized housing, then the distribution of subsidized and nonsubsidized housing is separated by income.

Symbolically, the index D_s of income separation of subsidized low-rent housing in a PHA is represented

$$D_s = \frac{1}{2} \sum_{i}^{N} | S_i - P_i | \tag{3}$$

where S_i is the proportion of the PHA's subsidized housing located in income area i, P_i is the proportion of the PHA's nonsubsidized housing in income area i, and N is the number of income areas in the PHA.

If every income area in the PHA has equal proportions of the jurisdiction's subsidized and nonsubsidized housing, the value of D_s will be at its minimum, 0. If the jurisdiction's subsidized and nonsubsidized housing are unequally represented in some or all income areas, the index D_s will have a value greater than 0. If the jurisdiction's subsidized and nonsubsidized housing are never located in the same income area, the value of D_s will be at its maximum, 1.

To illustrate how the index D_s of income separation is applied, consider the hypothetical data for two PHAs (PHA 1 and PHA 2), both containing two income areas, presented in Table 4.2. In each PHA, income area A is the low-income area, and income area B the moderate-high-income area. The hypothetical distribution of subsidized and nonsubsidized housing among the two income areas of PHA 1 and PHA 2 is shown in the table.

For each PHA, the percentage of subsidized housing is calculated by dividing the number of subsidized housing units in each area by the total number of subsidized housing units in the PHA. The percentage of nonsubsidized housing is calculated by dividing the number of nonsubsidized housing units in each area by the total number of nonsubsidized housing units in the PHA.

The values of the index D_s of income dispersal of subsidized housing (deviations) shows that the distribution of the subsidized and nonsubsidized housing among income areas is even for PHA 2 but not for PHA 1.

Data on Income Dispersal. While considerable data exist on public housing, their suitability for statistical study of this sort is limited. Two widely used sources of data on subsidized housing dispersal are the *Annual* or, later, *American Housing Survey* (AHS) and archives of federal and local housing authorities. Both have limitations. The AHS does not clearly distinguish among the different federal, state, and municipal housing subsidy programs, making it impossible to isolate these components and thereby allow for the great regional variation in state and municipal housing programs. Also, no distinction is made in the AHS between the family and elderly subprograms of federal housing. Nevertheless, the AHS provides useful comparisons with nonsubsidized housing, discussed in more detail below. Data from federal and local housing authorities, on the other hand, are reported by type of housing subsidy programs but provide little information on the economic characteristics of residential areas surrounding housing projects. The 1977 survey of PHAs, for example, merely reported the distribution of subsidized housing units between central-city and noncentral-city areas, and even this somewhat ambiguous distinction was reported unevenly.

Table 4.2
**Hypothetical Distribution of Subsidized and Nonsubsidized
Buildings by Income Areas**

Income Areas	Subsidized Units	Non-Subsidized Units	% Subsidized	% Non-Subsidized	Deviations
PHA 1					
Area A	750	1,800	60	10	-50
Area B	500	16,200	40	90	50
Total	**1,250**	**18,000**	–	–	–
PHA 2					
Area A	800	6,000	20	20	0
Area B	3,200	24,000	80	80	0
Total	**4,000**	**30,000**	–	–	–

Moreover, the available information on the location of subsidized low-rent housing projects is not consistent over time. Sites for low-rent housing projects were often obtained by demolishing low-income areas or slums, defined in the Housing Act of 1937 as "any area where dwellings predominate which, by reason of dilapidation, overcrowding, faulty arrangements or design, lack of ventilation, light or sanitation facilities, or any combination of these factors, are detrimental to safety, health or morals."[6] Projects were also built on vacant lands, that is, sites not previously residential, such as obsolete industrial areas and railroad yards.[7] Thus, during these early years the economic characteristics of areas surrounding low-rent housing projects were implied by the terminology used: *slum clearance* or *vacant site* projects.[8]

Somewhat later, beginning around the late 1960s and early 1970s, data on subsidized housing dispersal began to be collected based on the geographic location of projects.[9] This new data collection methodology characterized housing projects located in urbanized areas as *metropolitan* and those located outside urbanized areas as *nonmetropolitan*. Metropolitan projects are further subdivided into *central-city* and *noncentral-city* projects. There is evidently much potential for confusion and ambiguity in these terms.

The American Housing Survey of 1984 represented the first explicit attempt, at least at the national level, to collect information on income and other economic characteristics of neighborhoods surrounding low-rent housing projects, but its economic information proved of limited use in the current study. The "neighborhood clusters" described by the AHS data were surveyed

for "special analyses of neighboring units and rural units," and were not randomly selected (as are the survey units themselves).[10] In addition, "publicly
owned or subsidized housing" in the AHS includes federal, state, and municipal low-rent housing subsidy programs.[11] The accuracy of the sample data on
subsidized housing depends critically on the ability of individual respondents
to properly classify their units as public or private and, if private, as subsidized or nonsubsidized.[12]

Measuring Income Dispersal in Practice

As the above discussion indicates, data on the distribution of subsidized
housing projects among income areas are quite limited. By restructuring the
available information around two analytically discrete income areas, however, estimates of the index of income dispersal can be derived. To this end,
the following assumptions are made:

1. PHAs were equally divided into two income areas: the moderate-high-income
   area (income area 1) and the low-income area (income area 2). Moreover, to sim-
   plify the analysis the distribution of the total nonsubsidized housing between the
   two income areas is even, with one-half of the units located in each income area.[13]

2. For the 1932–1964 period, slum clearance projects were located in income area 2,
   and vacant site projects were located in income area 2 if their sites were totally
   vacant (in this case the area's only residents are the tenants) or spatially contiguous to an existing low-income area.

3. For the post–1965 period, central-city projects were located in income area 2,
   noncentral-city and nonmetropolitan projects in income area 1.

Based on the above assumptions, the index D_s of income separation of
subsidized low-rent housing projects is estimated as follows:

$$D_s = \frac{1}{2} \sum_i^N | S_i - P_i | \qquad (4)$$

From the assumption of two income areas, $N = 2$. From the assumption of
equal proportion of the PHA's nonsubsidized housing between the two areas,
$P_i = 0.50$ for $i = 1, 2$. Substituting gives

$$D_s = \frac{1}{2} (|S_1 - 0.50| + |S_2 - 0.50|) \qquad (5)$$
$$S_1 \geq 0$$
$$S_2 \geq 0$$

Replacing S_1 by $1-S_2$ and rearranging gives

$$D_s = |S_2 - 0.50| \qquad (6)$$

The estimate D_s is substantially more conservative than the ideal discussed earlier in this chapter. The assumption that the total nonsubsidized housing in a PHA is equally divided between income areas 1 and 2 may not be realistic in most situations. However, given that income dispersal has been defined differently at different periods of time, and that current housing policies tend to make only a broad distinction between the central city and noncentral city, the assumption minimizes many irrelevant variabilities in the data and provide a yardstick against which efforts to increase the dispersal of subsidized low-income housing projects can be tested.[14]

Measuring Racial Separation in Principle

The racial composition of tenants in low-rent housing projects is more difficult to analyze and measure than might be expected. At any given time, the racial composition of a subsidized housing project may be affected by several complementary factors: deliberate differential selection and/or assignment of applicants by the local housing authority; racial differences in turnover rates; and racial differences in the demographic characteristics of applicants. We attempt to deal with these various sources of causation with two estimates, $I_{xpha(assign)}$ and $I_{xpha(admit)}$, of the index of racial segregation, both mathematically based on the index D of residential dissimilarity.

The selection of eligible applicants and their assignment to units is done by local housing authorities; households which have qualified for a given housing subsidy program but not yet been assigned to units form the waiting list.[15] (The length of the wait varies by locality and programs; in large PHAs, for example, the average wait for a suitable unit in family public housing or Section 8 Existing programs can be more than five years.) For any housing subsidy program, the racial composition of the waiting list—that is, of those who have qualified for public housing—depends on a number of objective factors. Since the income of an applicant is one of the primary factors affecting eligibility, members of a group with a disproportionately larger number (relative to the population) of income eligible families will, other things equal, constitute a correspondingly larger proportion of a subsidized housing waiting list. In particular, if the eligible population in the PHA is predominantly black, the waiting list may also be predominantly black.

In addition to economic factors, racial differences in the demographic characteristics of the eligible population can also affect the racial composition of waiting lists for various types of housing. For example, if a PHA's eligible white population is predominantly elderly and its eligible African-American population is not, then the waiting list for the elderly housing subsidy program in that PHA would be predominantly white. The waiting list for the family housing subsidy program, on the other hand, would be predominantly African-American without such a distribution being the result of discrimination.

We attempt to measure the equity of admission of applicants to the waiting list and subsidized housing through the index $I_{xpha(admit)}$ of racial discrimination. The subscript of the index is a reference to the admission of racial group X to the PHA's general waiting list (if a PHA maintains several waiting lists for the same housing subsidy program, the general waiting list will be the combination of the several lists). The racial composition of the general waiting list, and thus ultimately of the PHA's tenants, should closely reflect the racial composition of the demand for low-income housing assistance in the entire PHA. A significant deviation of the racial composition of the general waiting list from that of the underlying demand for the specified assistance program would suggest racial discrimination in access.

The assignment of units to those accepted to the waiting list is a distinct issue, and we attempt to measure the equity of the PHA's assignment policies with the index $I_{xpha(assign)}$ of racial segregation. The subscript of the index is a reference to the assignment to housing projects of applicants already on the waiting list. Whatever the composition of the general waiting list, the assignment of applicants to units will be racially neutral if the racial composition of tenants in each housing project reflects the racial composition of the list. A significant deviation of the racial composition of individual housing projects from that of the waiting list suggests racial discrimination in the assignment of housing to accepted applicants.

Given, therefore, the racial composition of the general waiting list, the expected proportion $P_{xj(expect)}$ of tenants from racial group X in housing project j is equal to the proportion $P_{x(waiting)}$ of households from group X on the waiting list. Therefore,

$$P_{xj(expect)} = P_{x(waiting)} \tag{7}$$

The value of $P_{x(waiting)}$ and those of each $P_{xj(expect)}$ is between 0 (which would indicate no members of racial group X in the waiting list) and 1 (which would reflect a waiting list comprised entirely of members of group X).

The actual (post-assignment) proportion $P_{xj(actual)}$ of group X in housing project j is derived from the racial composition of tenants in the project:

$$P_{xj(actual)} = \frac{N_{xj(actual)}}{N_j} \tag{8}$$

where $N_{xj(actual)}$ is the actual number of tenant households from racial group X in project j and N_j is the number of units in project j.

If the selection and assignment of applicants by the PHA is racially neutral, the proportions $P_{xj(expect)}$ and $P_{xj(actual)}$ will be identical within random margins of error; significant differences between the two would reflect selection and assignment procedures that are not racially neutral. We denote the difference between the actual and the expected proportions of tenants of group X in housing project j by

$$DIFF_{xj(\text{assign})} = W \left| P_{xj(\text{expect})} - P_{xj(\text{actual})} \right| \qquad (9)$$

Then the assignment index $I_{xpha(\text{assign})}$ of racial segregation is given by

$$I_{xpha(\text{assign})} = \frac{\sum_{j}^{M} N_j DIFF_{xj(\text{assign})}}{\sum_{j}^{M} N_j} \qquad (10)$$

where $DIFF_{xj(\text{assign})}$ and N_j are as above. This can be thought of as the proportion of units (or households) that would have to be reassigned by the housing authority to arrive at a racially neutral distribution of tenants among housing projects.

The admission of households to a PHA's subsidized housing is examined by the complementary admission index $I_{xpha(\text{admit})}$, calculated in a similar manner from differences between the proportion $P_{x(\text{demand})}$ of racial group X among all households in the PHA nominally eligible for subsidized housing and group X's actual proportion in each project. For housing project j this difference is

$$DIFF_{xj(\text{admit})} = \left| P_{xpha(\text{demand})} - P_{xj(\text{actual})} \right| \qquad (11)$$

Thus the admission index is given by

$$I_{xpha(\text{admit})} = \frac{\sum_{j}^{M} N_j DIFF_{xj(\text{admit})}}{\sum_{j}^{M} N_j} \qquad (12)$$

where $DIFF_{xj(\text{admit})}$ and N_j are as above.

Local indices $I_{xpha(\text{assign})}$ ($I_{xpha(\text{admit})}$) can be combined into a national index of racial segregation $I_{xn(\text{assign})}$ ($I_{xn(\text{admit})}$) of tenants in a housing subsidy program:

$$I_{xn(\text{assign})} = \frac{\sum_{t}^{M} I_{xphat(\text{assign})} Y_t}{\sum_{t}^{M} Y_t} \qquad (13)$$

where $I_{phat(assign)}$ is the index of racial segregation of tenants in the housing subsidy program in PHA t due to assignment, Y_t is the total number of units in the housing subsidy program in PHA t, and M is the total number of PHAs. The index $I_{xn(admit)}$ is calculated in an analogous manner. National level indices ($I_{xn(assign)}$ and $I_{xn(admit)}$) are weighted by the total number of units in each PHA to account for the unequal representation of units in different PHAs. For example, in 1982 the twenty-two largest of over 1,000 PHAs owned more than one-third of units in the public housing program; the New York City Housing Authority alone accounted for over 13 percent of public housing units.[16] By contrast, the roughly 1,000 small PHAs (each with fewer than 100 units) had less than 5 percent of all public housing units.[17]

To illustrate the separate effects of the processes of selection and assignment of households on the racial composition of housing projects in a PHA, consider a hypothetical PHA with 170 units in three public housing projects, A, B, and C. Suppose that housing project A contains sixty units; project B, eighty units; and C, thirty units.[18] Assume also that 70 percent of all households nominally eligible for public housing in this PHA are black and the remaining 30 percent are white; and that the racial composition of the waiting list is 60 percent black and 40 percent white. Finally, assume that the actual occupancy of housing projects A, B, and C is as shown in Part I of Table 4.3. Given the hypothetical proportions of each racial group in the waiting list and the demand for subsidized housing assistance, the corresponding expected proportions of African-Americans and whites in three public housing projects A, B, and C are shown in Parts II and III of the table.

We first illustrate the derivation of the assignment index $I_{xpha(assign)}$ for our hypothetical PHA. In this PHA the overall number of units allocated to each racial group, namely 102 units to African-American and 68 to white tenants, is consistent with the racial composition of the waiting list. However, the specific assignment led to the obvious segregation of tenants by race. In housing project A, units are occupied exclusively by black tenants. In housing projects B and C, units are occupied predominantly by white tenants. This form of racial segregation in subsidized housing is easily recognizable.[19]

Table 4.4 shows the actual and expected proportions of African-American and white tenants in each of the three public housing projects (i.e., $P_{bj(actual)}$, $P_{bj(expect)}$, and $P_{wj(actual)}$, $P_{wj(expect)}$, respectively, $j = A, B, C$) and the deviations $DIFF_{wj(assign)}$ and $DIFF_{bj(assign)}$.

By simple inspection of the actual and expected proportions of the two racial groups of tenants among projects it can be seen that to arrive at a racially neutral distribution in the PHA's housing program, twenty-four units in public housing project A would have to be shifted from African-American to white tenants, while fourteen units in B and ten in C must be shifted from whites to African-Americans.

Overall, forty-eight tenant households (28% of 170 households) would have to be reassigned to different projects to achieve racial neutrality in assignment. Substituting the appropriate values from Table 4.4 yields[20]

Table 4.3
Distribution of Units among Projects and Expected Number of Black Tenants

Units and Tenants	Projects			
	A	B	C	Total
Total number of units	**60**	**80**	**30**	**170**
PART I				
Actual black tenants	60	34	8	102
Actual white tenants	0	46	22	68
PART II				
Expected (from waiting list) black tenants	36	48	18	102
Expected (from waiting list) white tenants	24	32	12	68
PART III				
Expected (from demand) black tenants	42	56	21	119
Expected (from demand) white tenants	18	24	9	51

$$I_{bpha(assign)} = \frac{48}{170} = 0.28 \tag{14}$$

To illustrate the derivation of the admission index $I_{xpha(admit)}$ (which measures the effect of discrimination in access to the program) consider the same hypothetical PHA. A comparison of total units allocated to the two racial groups in Parts I and III of Table 4.3 shows that blacks as a group ended up with seventeen units fewer than would be prescribed under a nondiscriminatory access to the housing program. On the other hand, whites as a group received seventeen units more than their nondiscriminatory share. Substituting the appropriate values yields

$$I_{bpha(admit)} = \frac{17}{170} = 0.1 \tag{15}$$

Data on Racial Occupancy. Unfortunately, data on the racial composition of individual buildings are not available at the national level; what is available is largely project-based racial occupancy data. No useful information on the racial composition of PHA waiting lists or the underlying demand for subsidized housing is available. These data limitations lead to modifications in the estimation procedures.

Table 4.4
Derivation of P'_{xj}, P_{xj}, and $DIFF_{xj}$ for White (w) and Black (b) Tenants

| Housing Projects | Total Units | Expected Units | | Actual | | Proportion | | Deviations | |
		Black	White	Black	White	Black[a] $P_{bj(actual)}$	White[a] $P_{wj(actual)}$	Black $DIFF_{bj(assign)}$	White $DIFF_{wj(assign)}$
A	60	36	24	60	0	1.00	0.00	+0.40	-0.40
B	80	48	32	34	46	0.42	0.57	-0.18	+0.18
C	30	18	12	8	22	0.27	0.73	-0.33	+0.33
Total	170	102	68	102	68	1.69	1.30	-0.11	+0.11

[a]The subscripts *wj* and *bj* are for *w*hite and *b*lack tenants, respectively.

During the early period of subsidized housing (1932–1964), racial composition information for individual housing projects was collected by the federal government using various definitions of race.[21] Often, particularly in the South, projects were built for and occupied exclusively by tenants of one race. When all projects in a PHA are racially homogeneous in this manner, the determination of $I_{xpha(assign)}$ is relatively simple. However, many PHAs had a third category of "racially mixed" or "racially integrated" projects, only a few of which had actual mixing of tenants of different races; the majority of these separated the races within the projects by building (or wing).[22] In general, the concept of racial integration and the collection of racial occupancy information evolved over time. Later classification schemes appear to be more detailed than earlier ones, but the concepts of "integration" and "segregation" were used with wide latitude. Indeed, these and other inconsistencies in the operational definition of "racial segregation" in low-rent housing were characteristics of early-period occupancy information.

The racial composition of waiting lists is unrecorded in general. The racial composition of families in substandard dwelling units in PHAs (the population most likely to be eligible for low-income housing assistance) is a good proxy, but the various available studies of housing conditions are not consistent enough in scope or focus to provide usable information. A second potential substitute is the racial composition of the poverty population in PHAs, since it is reasonable to expect the racial composition of the waiting list for housing assistance to reflect this closely; but such data are not available for the early periods, having first been collected in 1969.[23]

Modern (post–1964) information on racial occupancy is similarly available mostly in aggregate, project-based form, with no information on the racial composition of waiting lists or the underlying demand. Each new housing subsidy program seemingly was accompanied by its own set of forms for reporting tenant characteristics, resulting in a proliferation of parallel and duplicative forms and reporting systems.[24] However, reasonable project-based racial occupancy data are available for 1977. A new Multifamily Tenant Characteristics System (MTCS) introduced in 1992 by the Department of Housing and Urban Development has allowed the collection of consistent racial occupancy information on, currently, about 50 percent of subsidized housing units since that time. The 1977 survey and the MTCS data provide detailed project-based racial occupancy data in nearly all large metropolitan areas. These sources provide the most complete racial occupancy data available for the modern period.

The most consistent data available for the period 1930–1990 are for the PHA-wide proportions of racial groups and, from the census, for the racial composition of household units in cities with total populations of 50,000 or more. Consequently we will use a racial group's share of tenants and share of all households in a PHA as proxies for the proportion of the group in the general waiting list and the underlying demand, respectively. One limitation of the measure of discrimination is that it implicitly assumes that factors affecting applicant eligibility for low-income housing are equally spread across racial groups. In reality, in most PHAs African-Americans and other racial minorities often have relatively greater need of low-income housing assistance than their white counterparts, so the index of discrimination tends to understate the level of racial inequity.

Estimates of the Index of Racial Segregation in Practice

Two estimates $I'_{xpha(\text{assign})}$ and $I'_{xpha(\text{admit})}$ are made of the indices of racial segregation $I_{xpha(\text{assign})}$ and $I_{xpha(\text{admit})}$ described above. The first estimate, $I'_{xpha(\text{assign})}$, is calculated by comparing the racial composition of tenants in individual housing projects to the PHA-wide racial composition of all tenants. The second estimate, $I'_{xpha(\text{admit})}$, is calculated by comparing the racial composition of tenants in individual housing projects with the PHA-wide racial composition of all households, including nontenants. The two estimates of the index of racial segregation are mathematically analogous. If the PHA both selects and assigns applicants in a racially neutral manner and if the PHA-wide share of racial group X in households is proportional to group X's actual demand for low-income housing assistance, then both estimates should be low. Conversely, if the PHA selects or assigns tenants in a discriminatory fashion so that the proportion of tenants from racial group X in individual housing projects is significantly different from the overall share of group X among tenants or potential tenants, it will be reflected in higher values of one or both of the estimates.

To derive the estimate $I'_{xpha(\text{assign})}$ we set the expected proportion $P_{xj(\text{expect})}$ of households from group X in housing project j equal to the share $T_{x(\text{expect})}$ of group X among all the PHA's tenant households. $T_{x(\text{expect})}$ is a proxy for $P_{x(\text{waiting})}$, the proportion of racial group X on the PHA's general waiting list,

$$T_{x(expect)} = P_{x(waiting)} \tag{16}$$

The actual proportion $P_{xj(actual)}$ of tenants from racial group X in housing project j is

$$P_{xj(actual)} = \frac{N_{xj(actual)}}{N_j} \tag{17}$$

where $N_{xj(actual)}$ is the number of households from group X in housing project j, and N_j is the total number of households in housing project j. The absolute deviation $DIFF'_{x(assign)}$ is

$$DIFF'_{x(assign)} = |T_{x(expect)} - P_{xj(actual)}| \tag{18}$$

where $T_{xj(expect)}$ and $P_{xj(actual)}$ are as above. The first estimate $I'_{xpha(assign)}$ of segregation for racial group X can now be expressed as:

$$I'_{xpha(assign)} = \frac{\sum_j^M N_j DIFF'_{xj(assign)}}{\sum_j^M N_j} \tag{19}$$

where N_j is the total number of units in housing project j, M is the total number of housing projects in the PHA, and $DIFF'_{xj(assign)}$ is as above.

The difference between the theoretical index $I_{xpha(assign)}$ and its estimate $I'_{xpha(assign)}$ depends on the difference between the expressions $DIFF_{xj(assign)}$ and $DIFF'_{xj(assign)}$, the deviations of the actual proportion of PHA tenants of racial group X from, respectively, their expected proportion derived from the waiting list and their share among all tenants in the PHA.

The second estimate $I'_{xpha(admit)}$ is calculated analogously. In this case $T_{x(demand)}$, the proportion of households from racial group X in the total demand for subsidized housing assistance, is proxied by the PHA-wide racial composition of all households (tenants and nontenants). Formally,

$$T_{x(demand)} = P_{xj(demand)} \tag{20}$$

The actual proportion $P_{xj(actual)}$ of tenants from racial group X in housing project j is as above.

The absolute deviation $DIFF'_{xj(admit)}$ is

$$DIFF'_{xj(admit)} = |T_{x(expect)} - P_{xj(actual)}| \tag{21}$$

where $T_{xj(expect)}$ and $P_{xj(actual)}$ are as above. The second estimate $I'_{xpha(admit)}$ of segregation for racial group X can now be expressed as:

$$I'_{xpha(\text{admit})} = \frac{\sum\limits_{j}^{M} N_j DIFF'_{xj(\text{admit})}}{\sum\limits_{j}^{M} N_j} \qquad (22)$$

where N_j is the total number of units in housing project j, M is the total number of housing projects in the PHA, and $DIFF'_{xj(\text{admit})}$ is as above.

National-level first and second estimates $I'_{xn(\text{assign})}$ and $I'_{xn(\text{admit})}$ of the indices of racial segregation of tenants can be expressed as the weighted average of indices in individual PHAs, with more weight given to PHAs with more units.

Variations in Income and Racial Segregation

A formal test of the impact of the Civil Rights Act of 1964 on racial segregation and income separation is possible using the estimates $I'_{xn(\text{assign})}$ and $I'_{xn(\text{admit})}$ of the indices of racial segregation and the index D_s of income separation. A simple test is to compare the average value of each estimate or index in the two periods (before and after 1964).

The analysis of trends in the level of income separation will be performed for selected years between 1932 and 1992. The program of low-income housing and the number of PHAs has increased over time. Housing authorities, such as Chicago, Boston, New York City, and Atlanta, which were involved in the subsidized housing program before the Housing Act of 1937, were joined by others, such as Los Angeles, Dallas, and Baltimore, which were established later.

Given the severe limitations of the available data, and especially of comparable data over time, the outcome of statistical tests of hypotheses should be considered indicative rather than definitive. For instance, since our definition of income areas classifies noncentral-city housing projects as located in the moderate-high-income area, changes in the mean of the index of income separation (D_n) could simply reflect an accelerating trend toward the suburbanization of housing, rather than a qualitative shift in the distribution of subsidized low-rent housing projects among income areas. Such a test is also likely to bypass the role of cyclical economic growth and change in the central city. For example, some housing projects may be located in neighborhoods that were low income when the projects were constructed but have since been gentrified. In short, the relation between the civil rights and fair housing legislation and the income dispersal of subsidized low-rent housing cannot be fully captured with this simple statistical test.

A companion test of equality of the means of indices of racial segregation in low-income housing (I_{xn}) for the periods 1932–1964 and 1965–1992 is performed similarly. For each of the two estimates $I'_{xn(\text{assign})}$ and $I'_{xn(\text{admit})}$ of the index of racial segregation, if the mean for the early period is significantly higher than the mean for the modern period, it can be concluded that the civil rights and fair housing legislation contributed to the reduction in the level of racial segregation and discrimination in the low-income housing program. If the mean of the two estimates of the index (I_{xn}) for the early period is not significantly different from the mean of the estimates for the modern period, it can be concluded that the civil rights and fair housing legislation have had little or no effect on the level of racial segregation and discrimination in subsidized low-income housing. It is not expected that the indexes would be higher for the modern period.

This test, like the one for income separation, has certain limitations. In the early period, low-rent public housing for families was the only federally subsidized housing program available to the eligible population. In the modern period, members of the eligible population could choose among an increasingly large number of housing subsidy programs each tailored to the needs of a particular clientele. Some of these housing subsidy programs like the Section 23 Leased Housing and the Section 8 Housing Assistance Program were, in part, designed explicitly to reduce the level of tenant segregation by race.

The values of the second estimate of the index of racial segregation are based on data on the racial composition of households in PHAs with a total population of 50,000 or more. This means that the pattern of racial occupancy of housing projects in smaller PHAs is not taken into account in our comparative analysis.

Since a single composite index of racial segregation is calculated for diverse groups of housing subsidy programs, its complexities may make a simple comparison difficult. The results should be taken as indicative rather than definitive due to the imperfections in the data. However, since every effort has been made to render the index estimates conservative (i.e., counter to the hypotheses under consideration), some confidence can be placed in any positive outcome of the statistical tests.

SUMMARY

In analyzing segregation in subsidized low-income housing, the question of racial occupancy patterns should be clearly distinguished from that of income dispersal. Income dispersal refers to the distribution of housing projects among income areas in the PHA. Racial occupancy refers to the distribution of racial groups of tenants across housing projects. Together, income dispersal and racial occupancy constitute the two dimensions of segregation in a subsidized low-income housing program.

For a given pattern of income dispersal of housing projects there are potentially several patterns of racial occupancy. Subsidized housing projects could be uniformly distributed among existing income areas in a PHA but remain racially segregated in occupancy. Similarly, for a given pattern of racial occupancy, there are potentially several patterns of income dispersal. In principle, individual projects could be racially integrated in occupancy but concentrated in one income area.

The index D_s of income dispersal of subsidized low-income housing can be calculated in a manner analogous to the index D of residential dissimilarity.

Given the racial composition of the demand for a housing subsidy program and the composition of the general waiting list, the separation of tenants by race in housing projects can be attributed to the selection and assignment of applicants by the PHA. If the PHA selects and assigns applicants to units independently of the race factor, the racial composition of individual housing projects should reflect the racial composition of both the underlying demand for assistance and the general waiting list of the PHA. Consequently, if the racial compositions of tenants of individual housing projects diverge significantly from those of the demand and of the general waiting list, this suggests racial discrimination by the PHA.

NOTES

1. Another, less visible but important, form of segregation is the siting of housing projects by income levels of potential receiving neighborhoods.

2. Elizabeth C. Warren, "Measuring the Dispersal of Subsidized Housing in Three Cities," *Journal of Urban Affairs* 8 (1986).

3. Note this definition excludes the systemwide disparities in racial access to subsidized low-rent housing except insofar as they are reflected in unit by unit inequality.

4. It is, of course, possible for a PHA to be racially and economically integrated, and some racial groups still suffer inequity if access to the program for them is restricted by discrimination.

5. See Karl E. Taeuber, "Negro Residential Segregation: Trends and Measurement," *Social Problems* 12, 1 (1964): 44–45. It should be remembered that the index makes no distinction between voluntary associations and forced (legal or economic) segregation.

6. Helen B. Shaffer, "Slum Clearance: 1932–1952," *Editorial Research Report* 11, 20 (1952): 806–807.

7. Herbert J. Gans, "Human Implications of Current Redevelopment and Relocation Planning," *Journal of the American Institute of Planners* (February 1959): 15–25.

8. Although the term *blighted area* has not been precisely defined by the 1937 housing act, it usually refers to deserted industrial and commercial areas. See, for example, Shaffer, "Slum Clearance: 1932–1952," 807.

9. From the data collected it was impossible to answer the question whether the federal policy of site selection was properly implemented. See Richard Stuart Fleisher, "Subsidized Housing and Residential Segregation in American Cities: An Evaluation of the State Selection and Occupancy of Federally Subsidized Housing" (Ph.D. diss., University of Illinois at Urbana-Champaign, 1979), 3.

10. Abt Associates, Inc., *Codebook for the Annual Housing Survey Data Base*, prepared by Louise Hadden and Mireille Leger (Cambridge, Mass.: Abt Associates, Inc., 1988), 1.

11. Ibid., 111.

12. The following four questions were asked in the 1985 survey: (1) "Is the building owned by a public housing authority?" (2) "Does the federal government pay some of the cost of the unit?" (3) "Does the state or local government pay some of the cost of the unit?" (4) "Do (you/the people living here) have to report the household's income to someone every year so they can set rent?" Since federal, state, and municipal subsidized low-rent housing programs are administered in similar manners (often by the same local agency), the distinction between federal and local programs is not obvious from these questions.

13. This assumption is necessary because of data limitations.

14. For a predetermined proportion of the PHA's subsidized housing in the low-income area (S_2), the index D_s will underestimate the actual level of income separation if the proportion of the PHA's nonsubsidized housing in the low-income area (P_2) is less than 50 percent. The index D_s will overestimate the actual level of income separation if the proportion of the PHA's nonsubsidized housing in the low-income area is greater than 50 percent. In general, however, since the maximum admission income in subsidized low-rent housing will always be lower than the local median income, the low-income area in most PHAs will be smaller than the moderate-high-income area. As a result, the proportion of a PHA's nonsubsidized housing in the low-income area will often be lower than 50 percent. Therefore, the index will tend to understate rather than overstate the actual level of income separation in the PHA.

15. A suitable unit is a housing unit the occupancy of which by the tenant and his family will not result in overcrowding as defined in the Housing Quality Standard (HQS).

16. National Association of Housing and Redevelopment Officials, *This Is Public Housing* (Washington, D.C.: National Association of Housing and Redevelopment Officials, January 1988), n.p.

17. Congressional Budget Office, *Federal Subsidies for Public Housing: Issues and Options* (Washington, D.C.: U.S. Government Printing Office, June 1983). During World War II, two cities in California (Los Angeles and San Francisco) had nearly one-third of the public war housing units. If war housing units in Virginia, Washington, Illinois, Pennsylvania, and Ohio are added to the units in California, nearly three-quarters of units in the War Housing Program would be accounted for.

18. For the purpose of this discussion it is assumed that there are no significant racial differences in the demand for one, two, or three bedroom units, and so forth.

19. A more elaborate discussion would be based on the racial composition of the demand for units of given size. Thus, if 40 percent of all applicants in need of a one bedroom apartment are white and 60 percent black, the expected racial composition of any building with available one bedroom units should be 60 percent black and 40 percent white.

20. Since the example assumed only two racial groups of tenants in the PHA, the same result could be obtained using the distribution of African-American tenants among housing projects. Thus the index of racial segregation I_{xpha} will be the same for the two racial groups.

21. Charles Abrams, for example, classified public housing projects into the following groups:

1. *Insulated homogeneous*, that is, projects occupied by whites and Negroes separated into different areas.

2. *Insulated biracial*, that is, projects occupied by whites and Negroes in different sections of the same project.

3. *Mixed token*, that is, occupied predominantly by whites with a token Negro family to indicate absence of intentional discrimination.

4. *Mixed equal*, that is, occupied both by whites and Negroes in equal or nearly equal proportion.

5. *Mixed minority*, that is, occupied by whites predominantly but with Negroes represented by a minority.

6. *Insulated biracial–token*, that is, projects in which Negroes are predominantly separate within the project but with one or a few token Negro families mixed in with whites.

The author noted that the "most successful projects have been those with heterogeneous occupancy but in which the Negro tenants were sufficient in number to give them the self-assurance an ostracized race requires for its comfort." See Charles Abrams, "Living in Harmony; Mixed Housing, A Proving Ground," *Opportunity* (July, 1946): 116.

22. In their study of race relations in public housing, Deutsch and Collins classified all jointly occupied housing projects in which black and white tenants were assigned "separate sections or separate buildings" as *segregated biracial* housing projects. Housing projects in which "Negroes and whites were assigned to apartments anywhere . . . without regard to their race," were classified as *integrated interracial* housing projects (15). See Morton Deutsch and Mary Evans Collins, " Interracial Housing: A Survey of Opinion among Housing Officials," *Journal of Housing* (January, 1950): 14–16, 24. It should be noted that in this classification, no distinction was made between housing projects with different levels of participation of racial groups.

23. In practice, poverty alone has not been the final criterion of eligibility for a federal housing assistance program. Under the Housing Division of the PWA, only "self-sustaining workers" and their families were considered as potential tenants of public housing projects. Because of "high credit risks," low-income families and individuals on WPA and other forms of social relief were considered to be ineligible for assistance. During World War II, the program of public housing in nearly every PHA was made available to "immigrant defense workers." Again, during that period a large portion of the poverty population outside the defense program was ineligible for public housing. After World War II, the priority in admission to public housing was given to "large families with children" and "families displaced" by urban renewal and other government activities. The remainder of the poverty population, particularly single individuals and small families not displaced, were generally not eligible for public housing assistance. To review their history in detail, see National Housing Conference, *Housing Yearbook* (Washington, D.C.: National Housing Conference, annual, 1941–1968).

24. National Housing Conference, *Housing Yearbook* (Washington, D.C.: National Housing Conference, annual, 1941–1968).

5

Patterns of Segregation in Low-Income Housing, 1932–1963

Having explored the concept and measurement of segregation in low-income housing, we now turn to a detailed review of the patterns of segregation in federally subsidized housing from 1932 to 1963. As this review will show, housing assistance for the poor in the United States has consistently been characterized by racial and economic segregation. Individual buildings and projects were segregated by race in nearly all PHAs. During World War II, African-Americans and other racial minorities often were denied units in federally subsidized housing projects as a matter of public policy. The facilities were generally concentrated in neighborhoods with high poverty rates.

PATTERNS OF SEGREGATION UNDER THE PWA, 1932–1938

Between 1934 and 1937, the Public Works Administration (PWA) contracted for 51 housing projects containing 21,640 units in 36 cities.[1] Forty-nine of these projects were built in the continental United States, the other 2 in Puerto Rico and the U.S. Virgin Islands.[2] By 1937, 21 of the 49 continental projects (with 10,642 units, or 49% of all units) were occupied exclusively by white tenants and 15 (with 5,852, or 27%) exclusively by African-American tenants, while 7 (with 1,527, or 7%) were racially mixed or rather bisected, with tenants assigned by race to separate buildings or wings, and only 6 (with 3,290 units, or 15%) were racially integrated.[3]

The degree of integration varied among the six projects, African-Americans occupying six units of 294 and ten of 650 in two projects (in Cambridge, Mass.[4] and Cleveland,[5] respectively) but making up about half the tenants in three others (in Cincinnati, Cleveland, and Minneapolis). The seven bisected projects were in the North (Lackawanna, N.Y.; Milwaukee; Omaha; and Wayne, Pa.)[6] as well as the South (Columbia, S.C., and Lexington, Ky.). Analytically they differed very little from (officially) racially homogeneous projects, as can be seen from the Housing Authority of Omaha's description of such a project there, which "consists of both white and black occupants and there are 284 units. There is no distinct segregation of the whites from the blacks but individual buildings will be confined to either Negro or white."[7]

In the North as well as the South, local advisory committees on housing and the federal Housing Division itself were instrumental in creating or reinforcing racially segregated patterns of occupancy in the federal housing program. In Milwaukee, for example, tenants were separated by race at the request of the Housing Division and the Milwaukee Advisory Committee on Housing.[8] In Omaha and in Wayne, Pennsylvania, housing projects initially built for occupancy without reference to race were in actual operation either racially homogeneous or bisected. In Chicago, a project built in a previously integrated neighborhood was occupied exclusively by white tenants by 1938.

Estimates of the admission index $I'_{xpha(admit)}$ and the assignment index $I'_{xpha(assign)}$ were calculated for the 1937 PWA public housing. The case of Chicago is illustrative (see Table 5.1). African-Americans occupied none of the 2,414 units in the three PWA projects there, so the assignment index estimate $I'_{xpha(assign)}$, which is based on comparing the racial breakdowns of individual projects with that of the whole system, is trivially 0. There was no segregation of blacks within the system because there were no blacks within the system. This latter circumstance, of course, probably resulted from discrimination. It is quantified by the admission index $I'_{xpha(admit)}$, which is based on comparing the racial breakdowns of all households, tenants and nontenants (a proxy for the racial composition of the demand for subsidized housing assistance in the PHA), to those in individual projects.[9] In Chicago, whites comprised 80 percent of all households in 1930, African-Americans 6 percent, and "other" groups 14 percent. Thus the deviations $DIFF'_{w1(admit)}$, $DIFF'_{w2(admit)}$, $DIFF'_{w3(admit)}$) for whites are all equal to 0.20, those ($DIFF'_{b1(admit)}$, $DIFF'_{b2(admit)}$, $DIFF'_{b3(admit)}$) for blacks, 0.06. Therefore, the estimate is:

$$I'_{wpha(admit)} = \frac{925 * 0.20 + 462 * 0.20 + 1027 * 0.20}{2414} = 0.20 \qquad (23)$$

This suggests that the Chicago PHA discriminated in its admission policies, with whites as a group receiving about 483 (20% of the total) more units than their share in households. Of these 483 units, blacks would have received

Table 5.1
Pattern of Racial Occupancy and Index of Racial Segregation of Tenants in PWA Projects in the Housing Authority of Chicago, 1938

Housing Projects	Total Units	Occupied by		PHA-wide Proportion		Actual Proportion		Deviation (DIFF'$_{xi}$)		Units to be Reassigned	
		Whites	Blacks	Whites	Blacks	Whites	Blacks	Whites	Blacks	Whites	Blacks
Julia Lathrope Homes	925	925	0	1.00	0	1.00	0	0	0	0	0
Trumbull Park	462	462	0	1.00	0	1.00	0	0	0	0	0
Jane Addams Houses	1,027	1,027	0	1.00	0	1.00	0	0	0	0	0
Total	**2,414**	**2,414**	**0**	**1.00**	**0**	-	-	-	-	**0**	**0**

Source: Data from *Projects Files*.

about 145 units (6% of the total) had there not been racial discrimination in access to units.

The two estimates $I'_{xpha(assign)}$ and $I'_{xpha(admit)}$ were computed for each of 36 PHAs. Table 5.2 shows the total number of units, the PHA-wide proportion $T_{b(expect)}$ of African-Americans among households in each housing project, and the deviation $DIFF'_{bj}$ for the 49 PWA projects in 36 cities in the continental United States.[10] Table 5.3 shows the second estimate $I'_{xpha(admit)}$ of the index of racial segregation for selected PHAs.

Table 5.2
Estimate of the Assignment Index of Racial Segregation of Tenants in 49 PWA Projects, 1938

PHA	Housing Projects	Units	Racial Pattern[a]	Expected Black	Actual Black	$DIFF'_{bj(assign)}$
Atlanta, GA	Techwood Homes	604	W	0.53	0.00	0.53
Atlanta, GA	University Homes	675	B	0.53	1.00	0.47
Atlantic City, NJ	Stanley Holmes Village	277	B	1.00	1.00	0.00
Birmingham, AL	Smithfield Court	540	B	1.00	1.00	0.00
Boston, MA	Old Harbor Village	1,016	W	0.00	0.00	0.00
Buffalo, NY	Kenfield	658	W	0.00	0.00	0.00
Cambridge, MA	New Towne Court	294	M	0.02	0.02	0.00
Camden, NJ	Westfield Acres	514	W	0.00	0.00	0.00
Charleston, SC	Meeting Street Manor	112	W	0.47	0.00	0.47
Charleston, SC	Cooper River Court	100	B	0.47	1.00	0.53
Chicago, IL	Julia Lathrope Homes	925	W	0.00	0.00	0.00
Chicago, IL	Trumbull Park	462	W	0.00	0.00	0.00
Chicago, IL	Jane Addams Houses	1,027	W	0.00	0.00	0.00
Cincinnati, OH	Laurel Homes	1,039	M	0.47	0.47	0.00
Cleveland, OH	Lakeview Terrace	620	W	0.29	0.00	0.28
Cleveland, OH	Cedar Central Apts	650	M	0.29	0.02	0.27
Cleveland, OH	Outhwaite Homes	579	M	0.29	0.97	0.68
Dallas, TX	Cedar Spring Place	181	W	0.00	0.00	0.00
Detroit, MI	Parkside	775	W	0.47	0.00	0.47
Detroit, MI	Brewster	701	B	0.47	1.00	0.53
Enid, OK	Cherokee Terrace	80	W	0.00	0.00	0.00
Evansville, IN	Lincoln Gardens	191	B	1.00	1.00	0.00

In general, the patterns of racial occupancy of PWA projects show no consistent relations with the racial shares of public housing tenants, of total PWA households, or of the PWA poverty population.[11] But discrimination is often plain; for example, if tenants had been selected based on their need for public housing alone, then the share of African-Americans in public housing in Philadelphia and Chicago would be significantly larger than zero (and probably larger than their share in the general population. Based on incomplete estimates of the poverty population between 1932 and 1937, up to 70 percent of the African-American population in Chicago and Philadelphia was on relief or WPA).[12]

Table 5.2 (*continued*)

PHA	Housing Projects	Units	Racial Pattern[a]	Expected Black	Actual Black	DIFF'$_{bj(assign)}$
Indianapolis, IN	Lockefield Garden	748	B	1.00	1.00	0.00
Jacksonville, FL	Durkeeville	215	B	1.00	1.00	0.00
Louisville, KY	Lasalle Place	210	W	0.37	0.00	0.37
Louisville, KY	College Court	125	B	0.37	1.00	0.63
Memphis, TN	Lauderdale Court	449	W	0.59	0.00	0.59
Memphis, TN	Dixie Homes	633	B	0.59	1.00	0.41
Miami, FL	Liberty Square	243	B	1.00	1.00	0.00
Minneapolis, MN	Sumner Field Homes	464	M	0.60	0.60	0.00
Montgomery, AL	Riverside Heights	100	W	0.61	0.00	0.61
Montgomery, AL	Wm. Paterson	156	B	0.61	1.00	0.39
Nashville, TN	Cheatham Place	314	W	0.56	0.00	0.56
Nashville, TN	Andrew Jackson	398	B	0.56	1.00	0.44
New York, NY	Williamsburg Homes	1,622	W	0.26	0.00	0.26
New York, NY	Harlem River Houses	576	B	0.26	1.00	0.74
Oklahoma City, OK	Will Roger Courts	354	W	1.00	1.00	0.00
Philadelphia, PA	Hill Creek	258	W	0.00	0.00	0.00
Schenectady, NY	Schonowee Village	219	W	0.00	0.00	0.00
Stamford, CT	Fairfield Court	146	W	0.00	0.00	0.00
Toledo, OH	Brand Whitlock	264	M	0.85	0.85	0.00
Washington, DC	Langston	274	B	1.00	1.00	0.00
U. S.		21,315	**Estimate of the Index I'$_{xpha(assign)}$ = 0.24**			

[a]Racial codes: W: all white B: all black M: racially mixed with no separation by buildings. For racially bisected projects (BS) the actual proportion of black tenants is for the black section of the project.

More generally, the values of the estimate $I'_{xpha(admit)}$ of the index suggest that 37 percent of all units in the PWA program should have been assigned to tenants from racial groups other than groups actually assigned. This estimate should be considered as the lower value of the actual level of racial segregation and discrimination since most factors affecting eligibility were ignored.

Table 5.3
Estimates of the Level of Racial Segregation in Admissions in Selected PHAs, 1938 (Based on the Share among Households)

PHA	Projects	Total Units		Total Households[a]		Estimates ($I'_{xpha(admit)}$)
		% Black	% White	% Black	% White	
Atlanta, GA	2	53.00	47.00	35.00	62.00	0.51
Birmingham, AL	1	100.00	0.00	41.00	58.00	0.58
Boston, MA	1	0.00	100.00	3.00	87.00	0.53
Buffalo, NY	1	0.00	100.00	2.00	62.00	0.05
Cambridge, MA	1	1.00	99.00	4.00	81.00	0.00
Camden, NJ	1	0.00	100.00	1.00	61.00	0.40
Chicago, IL	3	0.00	100.00	6.00	80.00	0.33
Cincinnati, OH	1	47.00	53.00	10.00	76.00	0.00
Cleveland, OH	3	0.00	100.00	8.00	87.00	0.18
Dallas, TX	1	0.00	100.00	16.00	78.00	0.22
Detroit, MI	2	47.00	53.00	7.00	83.00	0.50
Evansville, IN	1	100.00	0.00	7.00	89.00	0.89
Indianapolis, IN	1	100.00	0.00	12.00	81.00	0.82
Jacksonville, FL	1	100.00	0.00	37.00	56.00	0.57
Louisville, KY	2	37.00	63.00	17.00	77.00	0.50
Memphis, TN	2	59.00	41.00	43.00	53.00	0.22
Miami, FL	1	100.00	0.00	20.00	68.00	0.68
Milwaukee, WI	1	47.00	53.00	1.00	66.00	0.00
Minneapolis, MN	1	4.00	96.00	1.00	68.00	0.00
New York, NY	2	26.00	74.00	4.00	44.00	0.50
Philadelphia, PA	1	0.00	100.00	11.00	56.00	0.44
Toledo, OH	1	3.00	97.00	4.00	75.00	0.00
Washington, DC	1	100.00	0.00	24.00	66.00	0.67
U. S.	32		Estimate of the Index $I_{xpha(admit)}$		= 0.37	

[a]Percentages do not add up to 100 because of missing census data.

PATTERNS OF INCOME DISPERSAL UNDER THE PWA

Twenty-seven of the 49 housing projects built by the Housing Division of the PWA in 1937 were slum clearance projects located in low-income areas. The remaining 22 were vacant site projects, most located next to existing low-income areas.[13] In terms of economic conditions, vacant site housing projects, like clearance projects, were all located in low-income areas.

No attempt was made at either the federal or local level to diversify the location of PWA public housing projects.[14] Substantial cutbacks in the budget of the Housing Division (of $125 million earmarked for public housing under the Industrial Recovery Act of 1933, $94 million was rescinded the same year) reinforced the need for economy and the emphasis on relatively cheap sites in low-income neighborhoods and vacant areas.

Many cities used the experimental public housing program as a means for the displacement of inconveniently located low-income neighborhoods, especially those with African-American residents.[15] Techwood Homes in Atlanta was all too typical of this. Located near the Capitol Building of Georgia, this project was built in a predominantly "Negro section of town" which had been cleared by persuading the residents to sell their small properties in the name of "civic improvement." When the project was ready for occupancy the former residents of the site were disqualified by the Housing Division as "not good enough."[16] The result was the removal of the "Negro population" and its replacement by economically "self-sustaining" white families. According to the Capitol Planning and Housing Corporation of Atlanta in 1933,

For a great many years, the city of Atlanta has honestly endeavored to improve and beautify properties surrounding and adjacent to that of the Capitol Building of Georgia, and the City Hall of Atlanta. Unfortunately, heretofore it has been impossible to accomplish a project of this nature due to the fact that capital for this type of improvement was not available.

Due to the dilapidated conditions of a great many of the buildings in this particular area and general living conditions a certain amount of colored residents have crept into the white section, which of course has depreciated property values and eliminated the better type of white people who heretofore occupied this area. By the building of this project, the colored people will be eliminated and taken care of by other housing projects, which are now under way in the city.[17]

In Atlanta and throughout the nation, all projects being initially located in the low-income part of town, the national estimate of the index D_n of income separation takes on its maximum possible value of 0.50.

CONCLUSIONS ABOUT THE PWA

In sum, the experimental program of the Housing Division of the PWA of the 1930s was overwhelmingly segregated and totally separated by income. Housing projects were located exclusively in the low-income area. Tenants were segregated by race through either race-specific housing projects or explicit racial sections within projects. All but 6 of the 49 housing projects were segregated; and in 2 of the 6, less than 1 percent of the tenants in 1937 were African-American.

PATTERNS OF SEGREGATION UNDER THE USHA, 1938–1941

The USHA program maintained the racial segregation and income separation of its predecessor in the approximately 132,500 units in 163 housing projects built under its auspices between 1938 and 1941.[18] Of those, 35 percent were in housing projects occupied exclusively by African-American tenants, 21 percent were in housing projects occupied exclusively by white tenants, and 44 percent were in racially integrated housing projects—some of which were probably bisected rather than integrated.[19] A summary distribution by racial occupancy of the 261 projects is given in Table 5.4.[20] At least 236 of these were racially homogeneous, and only about 20 were racially mixed. (The racial composition of tenants in 5 housing projects is unknown. Note that fewer than 10% of the projects account for 44% of the total number of units.) The 236 homogeneous projects included 122 (containing 47% of the total units) occupied exclusively by white tenants, 106 (about 40% of the units) by African-American tenants, and 8 (3% of the units) by Hispanic tenants.

Table 5.4
Distribution of USHA Housing Projects by Racial Types, 1941

Racial Types of Projects	Total Projects	% of Total Units	By Regions		
			North	South	West
All White Occupancy	122	46.74	45	65	12
All Black Occupancy	106	40.61	28	76	2
All Latino Occupancy	8	3.06	0	7	1
Racially Mixed	20	7.66	16	0	4
Unknown Racial Occupancy	5	1.91	89	148	19
Total	**261**	**100**	**133**	**231**	**26**

Source: Federal Works Agency, United States Housing Authority, Research and Statistics Division, *Report R&S 15A* (December 6, 1941).

Just under one-half of housing projects in the North were occupied exclusively by white tenants.[21] In the South, all projects were racially homogeneous, 7 (6 in Texas and 1 in Florida) being occupied exclusively by Latino tenants, 76 by African-American tenants, and 64 by white tenants.

The racial barriers in the public housing in the South were so rigid that, for example, in 1942 when the Housing Authority of Charlotte, N.C., lost nearly one-quarter of its white tenants (who moved to other cities in search of defense employment) the units they left remained vacant despite many eligible African-American applicants.[22]

The two estimates $I'_{xpha(admit)}$ and $I'_{xpha(assign)}$ of the index of racial segregation were calculated for the USHA's program in 1941. To illustrate, consider the Housing Authority of Meridian, Mississippi, which then operated a total of 379 units in four housing projects.[23] Of these, 210 units (55 percent) were occupied by African-Americans and 169 (45%) by whites (see Table 5.5).

For each of the four housing projects, the deviation $DIFF'_{bj(assign)}$ ($DIFF'_{wj(assign)}$) of the proportion of black (white) tenants from the PHA-wide proportion straightforwardly calculates to an absolute value of $DIFF'_{j(assign)} = 0.554$ for the white-occupied projects (for whites $DIFF'_{wj(assign)} = 1 - 0.446 = 0.554$; for African-Americans $DIFF'_{bj(assign)} = 0 - 0.554 = -0.554$), and an absolute value of $DIFF'_{j(assign)} = 0.446$ (for whites $DIFF'_{wj(assign)} = 0 - 0.446 = -0.446$; for African-Americans $DIFF'_{bj(assign)} = 1 - 0.554 = 0.446$) for the black occupied. By multiplying the deviation $DIFF'_{j}$ by the total number of units in each of the four housing projects and then dividing the sum of these products by the total number of units in the PHA, we obtain the estimate $I'_{bpha(assign)}$ of the index of racial segregation, the assignment index:[24]

$$I'_{bpha(assign)} = \frac{187}{379} = 0.49 \tag{24}$$

In other words, to arrive at a neutral distribution of racial groups among Meridian's facilities, 187 units (49% of the PHA's public housing stock) would have had to be exchanged between African-American and white tenants.[25]

The indices are estimated similarly for the other USHA cities for 1941 (see Table 5.6). Again, we divide the PHAs into three groups: those in which at least one project was occupied jointly by different racial groups, called *racially integrated* PHAs; those with tenants from only one racial group; and those with tenants from at least two different racial groups which assigned them to separate housing projects.

Consider the first index for each of these categories. PHAs with different racial groups in separate housing projects were distributed throughout the nation, with an especially high concentration in the South. Among these PHAs some localities were more segregated than others. At times this may be misleading since the estimate $I_{xpha(assign)}$ measures only the proportion of units that must be exchanged between existing tenants to arrive at a racially even distri-

Table 5.5
Pattern of Racial Occupancy and Index of Racial Segregation of Tenants in USHA Projects in the Housing Authority of Meridian, 1941

Housing Projects	Total Units	Occupied by		PHA-wide Proportion		Actual Proportion		Deviation $(DIFF_{xj})$		Units to be Reassigned	
		Whites	Blacks	Whites	Blacks	Whites	Blacks	Whites	Blacks	Whites	Blacks
Highway Village	89	89	0	0.45	0.55	1.00	0.00	+0.55	-0.55	49	49
Mountain View	80	80	0	0.45	0.55	1.00	0.00	+0.55	-0.55	44	44
Frank Berry Ct.	113	0	113	0.45	0.55	0.00	1.00	-0.45	+0.45	50	50
George Reese Ct.	97	0	97	0.45	0.55	0.00	1.00	-0.45	+0.45	43	43
Total	**379**	**169**	**210**	**0.45**	**0.55**	-	-	-	-	**187**	**187**

Source: Data from *Projects Files*.

Table 5.6
Estimates of the Index of Racial Segregation for Selected PHAs, 1941

PHA	Estimates of Index I'$_{xpha(assign)}$			In Projects Occupied only by		
	White	Black	Hispanics	White	Black	Hispanics
Buffalo, NY	0.19	0.19	-	1,440	172	-
Huntington, WV	0.27	0.27	-	420	80	-
Detroit, MI	0.29	0.29	-	1,095	240	-
Birmingham, AL	0.33	0.33	-	1,776	480	-
Trenton, NJ	0.36	0.36	-	376	118	-
Elizabeth, NJ	0.37	0.37	-	628	200	-
Brownsville, TX	-	0.37	0.37	-	49	149
Phoenix, AR	0.47	0.37	0.47	230	150	224
Corpus Christi, TX	0.44	0.37	0.49	158	122	210
San Antonio, TX	0.45	0.38	0.48	796	578	932
Memphis, TN	0.38	0.38	-	478	1,400	-
Peoria, IL	0.39	0.39	-	1,333	487	-
West Palm Beach, FL	0.40	0.40	-	122	328	-
Augusta, GA	0.40	0.40	-	167	446	-
Bridgeport, CT	0.42	0.42	-	1,239	516	-
Lexington, KY	0.42	0.42	-	86	206	-
Athens, GA	0.42	0.42	-	54	126	-
Kingsport, TN	0.42	0.42	-	128	56	-
Long Branch, NJ	0.43	0.43	-	87	40	-
Columbus, OH	0.43	0.43	-	926	426	-
Charleston, SC	0.43	0.43	-	269	580	-
Knoxville, TN	0.43	0.43	-	244	520	-
Miami, FL	0.44	0.44	-	345	730	-
Savannah, GA	0.44	0.44	-	314	656	-
Biloxi, MS	0.44	0.44	-	192	96	-
Bristol, VA	0.44	0.44	-	136	68	-
Omaha, NB	0.45	0.45	-	522	272	-
Williamson, WV	0.45	0.45	-	72	38	-
Atlanta, GA	0.46	0.46	-	1,246	2,290	-
Mount Hope, WV	0.46	0.46	-	45	25	-
Charleston, WV	0.46	0.46	-	170	304	-
Washington, DC	0.46	0.46	-	543	313	-
Macon, GA	0.47	0.47	-	188	318	-

Table 5.6 (*continued*)

PHA	Estimates of Index $I_{xpha(assign)}$			In Projects Occupied only by		
	White	Black	Hispanics	White	Black	Hispanics
Paducah, KY	0.47	0.47	–	125	74	–
Baltimore, MD	0.47	0.47	–	701	1,125	–
Rome, GA	0.48	0.48	–	148	94	–
Toledo, OH	0.48	0.48	–	384	246	–
Columbus, GA	0.48	0.48	–	360	392	–
Austin, TX	0.50	0.48	0.21	162	130	40
Covington, KY	0.48	0.48	–	235	163	–
Spartanburg, MS	0.49	0.49	–	120	150	–
High Point, NC	0.49	0.49	–	250	200	–
Nashville, TN	0.49	0.49	–	386	480	–
Meridian, MS	0.49	0.49	–	169	210	–
Charlotte, NC	0.49	0.49	–	368	452	–
Tampa, FL	0.40	0.50	0.39	328	534	320
Laurel, MS	0.50	0.50	–	150	125	–
Alexandria, VA	0.50	0.50	–	130	110	–
Jacksonville, FL	0.50	0.50	–	600	708	–
Wilmington, NC	0.50	0.50	–	216	246	–
Chattanooga, TN	0.50	0.50	–	437	497	–
Brunswick, GA	0.50	0.50	–	128	144	–
Madisonville, KY	0.50	0.50	–	50	45	–
McComb, MS	0.50	0.50	–	84	76	–
Montgomery, AL	0.50	0.50	–	137	150	–
Columbus, GA	0.50	0.50	–	360	392	–
Harrisburg, PA	0.50	0.50	–	236	224	–
Phenix City, AL	0.50	0.50	–	216	206	–
Jackson, TN	0.50	0.50	–	100	96	–
Columbia, SC	0.50	0.50	–	236	244	–
Louisville, KY	0.50	0.50	–	786	808	–
Fort Worth, TX	0.50	0.50	–	252	250	–
Akron, OH	0.50	0.50	–	274	276	–
Pelly, TX	0.50	0.50	–	30	30	–
Pensacola, FL	0.50	0.50	–	120	120	–
Pittsburgh, PA	0.50	0.50	–	3,073	3,073	–
Raleigh, NC	0.50	0.50	–	231	231	–

bution in the PHA. For example, 1,440 of Buffalo's 1,612 units were in housing projects occupied exclusively by whites; the others were in a single housing project occupied exclusively by African-Americans. The extent of unit reassignment required to arrive at a neutral distribution of racial groups among housing projects, and consequently the estimate $I_{xpha(assign)}$, is relatively small, despite our intuitive sense of racial inequity of the actual situation. In contrast, fairly extensive unit reassignment would have been needed to arrive at a neutral distribution of racial groups among the housing projects of Akron or Pittsburgh or several other cities which were practically 50 percent white and 50 percent African-American.

PHAs with tenants drawn entirely from one racial group were also distributed throughout the nation, but with a particularly strong northern concentration. For these PHAs the value of the first estimate $I'_{xpha(assign)}$ is 0. Some, notably those in Montana, were all white because there were few or no potential African-American tenants in the PHAs. Others, including Asbury Park, New Jersey, and Gary, Indiana, housed only African-Americans (see Table 5.7). As with the earlier Chicago example, the 0 value for this index is misleading in many cases as racial groups were not segregated within the PHA because some had been kept outside entirely.

The racially integrated PHAs, those with one or more racially mixed housing project, were all in the North and West, and all had index values near or equal to 0. Most of these had only one project, so that their index values simply reflect the trivial deviation of 0. But the three PHAs with more than one integrated project also had very low, if nonzero, index values (see Table 5.8).

At least one of these cases seems genuinely significant. The deviation of the racial composition of tenants in three New York City housing projects[26] from the PHA-wide racial composition of tenants was less than 0.05.[27]

To investigate possible racial discrimination in admission to public housing the second index estimate $I'_{xpha(admit)}$, based on the shares of racial groups in households in the PHA, was calculated for PHAs with a total population of at least 50,000 people (see Table 5.9). Surprisingly, the aggregate values, using the two techniques, were quite similar, the first estimate being 0.31 and the second 0.33. The various weaknesses in the first index seem to have been offset at the national level.

The second estimate of the index suggests high levels of racial discrimination in the USHA's programs in some northern PHAs, including Chicago, Dayton, and Baltimore, as well as many in the South.

According to Federal Works Agency reports, there appears to have been a substantial amount of racial discrimination in the selection of applicants in many PHAs, although there was, overall, only a moderate amount of outright exclusion. As shown in Table 5.10, nearly 51 percent of all applicants eligible for public housing assistance were African-American, but less than 45 percent of all units in the program went to them.[28]

Table 5.7
PHAs with Only One Racial Group of Tenants, 1941

PHA	Number of Projects	Race of Tenants
Asbury Park, NJ	1	Black
Atlantic City, NJ	1	White
Camden, NJ	1	Black
Chester, PA	1	Black
Chicago, IL	1	Black
Cincinnati, OH	1	White
Cleveland, OH	2	White
Dayton, OH	1	Black
Delaware County, IN	1	White
Fort Wayne, IN	1	White
Frederick, MD	1	Black
Gary, IN	1	Black
Granite City, IL	1	White
Hammond, IN	1	White
Hartford, CT	2	White
Kokomo, IN	1	White
McKeesport, PA	1	White
New Bedford, MA	1	White
New Haven, CT	1	Black
North Bergen, NJ	1	White
Norwalk, CT	1	Black
Perth Amboy, NJ	1	White
Philadelphia, PA	1	Black
Portsmouth, OH	1	White
Reading, PA	1	White
Syracuse, NY	1	White

Table 5.7 (*continued*)

PHA	Number of Projects	Race of Tenants
Vincennes, IN	1	White
Warren, OH	2	Black
Youngstown, OH	1	White
Anniston, AL	1	White
Daytona Beach, FL	2	Black
El Paso, TX	2	Latino
Fort Lauderdale, FL	1	Black
Frankfort, KY	1	White
Hattiesburg, MS	1	Black
Hopewell, VA	1	Black
Houston, TX	3	Black
Kinston, NC	1	White
Lakeland, FL	1	Black
Laredo, TX	1	Latino
Martinsburg, WV	2	White
New Bern, NC	1	White
Newport News, VA	1	Black
Orlando, FL	2	Black
Sarasota, FL	1	Black
St. Petersburg, FL	2	Black
Wheeling, WV	1	White
Butte, MT	1	White
Denver, CO	1	White
Great Falls, MT	1	White
Helena, MT	1	White
Lomita, CA	1	White
Long Beach, CA	1	White
North Little Rock, AR	1	White
San Francisco, CA	3	White

Table 5.8
PHAs with Racially Mixed Housing
Projects, 1941

Name of PHA	Number of Projects	Race of Tenants
Allentown, PA	1	Mixed
Annapolis, MD	1	Mixed
Danville, IL	2	Mixed
Fall River, MA	1	Mixed
Harrison, NJ	1	Mixed
Kewanee, IL	1	Mixed
Muncie, IN	1	Mixed
New Britain, CT	1	Mixed
New York, NY	3	Mixed
Newark, NJ	4	Mixed
Springfield, IL	1	Mixed
Utica, NY	1	Mixed
Yonkers, NY	1	Mixed
Zanesville, OH	1	Mixed
Los Angeles, CA	1	Mixed
Oakland, CA	2	Mixed

In some PHAs, including Baltimore, Chicago, Philadelphia, Miami, and Houston, over 70 percent of applicants apparently eligible for housing assistance were African-American in 1941.[29] If racial groups of applicants were selected and assigned units in the same proportion as the racial composition of the eligible population, 58 percent of southern tenants and 45 percent of northern tenants would have been African-American in 1941; in fact, these figures were 54 percent and 40 percent, respectively (see Table 5.11).[30]

This comparison shows that African-Americans received fewer units than would be expected from the racial composition of the eligible population. Interestingly, the differences by region suggest that the South was closer to equity in the overall distribution of units than the North, where such PHAs as Newark and Buffalo maintained exclusionary policies which made it difficult for African-Americans to obtain public housing.[31]

Table 5.9
Estimates of the Index of Racial Segregation in Low-Rent
Housing by Regions and United States, 1941

				Estimates (I_n) Based on	
Region	Cities	Projects	Units	$I'_{xpha(assign)}$	$I'_{xpha(admit)}$
North	50	84	35,238	0.23	0.32
South	60	147	36,592	0.41	0.44
West	12	19	5,992	0.14	0.18
Total	**122**	**250**	**77,822**	**0.31**	**0.33**

Source: Based on data from Federal Works Agency, United States Housing
Authority, Research and Statistics Division, *Report R&S 15A* (December
6, 1941).

The USHA projects nevertheless seem more responsive to the needs of
low-income families in general (if not African-Americans specifically) than
those of the Housing Division of the PWA. In 1941, for the first time, "Persons on Relief, Pensions, etc." were accepted as tenants in public housing.[32]
This category included 14 of 168 families at a black housing project in Buffalo and 23 of 216 in a white housing project in Jacksonville. An immediate
effect of this new admission policy was an increase in the total share of blacks
in public housing from 35 percent in 1938 to 44 percent in 1941.[33]

Rents were also adjusted more closely to the incomes of tenants under the
USHA than under the PWA. In 1939, the USHA reduced rents in 24 housing
projects built by the Housing Division of the PWA.[34]

PATTERNS OF INCOME DISPERSAL UNDER THE USHA

In 1941, the USHA completed or contracted for 274 housing projects, with
53 percent sited in existing low-income residential areas and the remaining
47 percent targeted for vacant sites.[35] Like clearance projects, vacant-site
projects were located in low-income areas, usually old working-class districts or abandoned industrial parks or railroad yards.[36]

By income areas, 61,805 of 100,807 units (61%) were in housing projects
located in low-income areas.[37] The remaining 39,002 units (39%) were in
housing projects located on vacant sites which, as mentioned before, were all
low-income areas.[38] Like the program of the PWA, there was no significant
variation in the economic characteristics of areas surrounding housing projects
built by the USHA. The index of income separation (D_n) remained constant
and equal to its maximum value of 0.50.[39]

Table 5.10
Racial Composition of the Demand for Public Housing, 1941

Region	Race of Applicants	Applications Received		Apparently Eligible	
		Total	%	Total	%
U.S. Total	White	152,789	54.86	61,368	49.34
	Black	125,696	45.13	63,002	50.66
	Total	278,485	100.00	124,370	100.00
North	White	80,297	55.78	29,055	54.71
	Black	63,660	44.22	24,054	45.29
	Total	143,957	100.00	53,109	100.00
South	White	57,062	48.08	27,436	41.54
	Black	61,613	51.92	38,608	58.46
	Total	118,675	100.00	66,044	100.00
West	White	15,430	97.33	4,877	93.48
	Black	423	2.67	340	6.51
	Total	15,853	100.00	5,217	100.00

Source: Federal Works Agency, United States Housing Authority, Research and Statistics Division, *Report R&S 15A* (December 6, 1941).

Note: The number of applicants is for housing projects in which the pattern of occupancy by whites and blacks is known. Projects with only Latino tenants and projects with unknown racial occupancy were excluded.

CONCLUSIONS ABOUT THE USHA

In summary, under the United States Housing Authority, as under the PWA, public housing tenants were generally segregated by race, with African-Americans, whites, and Latinos usually, and always in the South, being assigned separate housing projects. As with the PWA, a primary goal of the USHA was to facilitate the removal of low-income families and individuals from areas adjacent to central business districts. Since housing projects were to be "designed and constructed for economy," properties in low-income neighborhoods or vacant areas became the most desirable sites of public housing.[40]

Racially, tenants were rarely mixed in the same buildings. In the South, in particular, whites were invariably assigned to white housing projects and African-Americans to Negro housing projects. In the North and West, the pat-

Table 5.11
Distribution of Units among Racial
Groups of Tenants in Public Housing,
1941

Region	Race of Tenants	Total Number of Units	
		Total[a]	%
U.S.	White	36,193	55.16
	Black	29,410	44.83
	Total	65,603	100.00
North	White	18,151	60.00
	Black	12,102	40.00
	Total	30,253	100.00
South	White	14,367	45.57
	Black	17,158	54.43
	Total	31,525	100.00
West	White	3,675	96.08
	Black	150	3.92
	Total	3,825	100.00

Source: Federal Works Agency, United States Housing Authority, Research and Statistics Division, *Report R&S 15A* (December 6, 1941).

[a]The total number of units is for housing projects occupied by white or black tenants.

terns were not significantly different. While a small number of housing projects in those regions were occupied jointly by whites and African-Americans, even some of these integrated projects were segregated by buildings or wing.

In terms of the overall distribution of units among racial groups, the program of the USHA was discriminatory despite some effort to make the units more affordable for minorities and lower-income families. In 1941, 51 percent of all applicants eligible for public housing assistance were African-Americans, but fewer than 45 percent of all units were actually assigned to them. Whites, who comprised 49 percent of the eligible applicants, received more than 55 percent of all units.

PATTERNS OF SEGREGATION IN WAR HOUSING, 1941–1945

The war housing programs were somewhat anomalous in the history of public housing since so much of the housing was temporary, but there was significant continuity in patterns of segregation and income isolation. The war programs also illustrate the possible scale of public housing if housing were actually the objective. Overall the total number of subsidized units made available to defense and defense-related workers increased from about 331,000 to 1.3 million units from 1941 to 1944. Unfortunately, only about 900,000 of those units were intended to be kept as public housing after the war; the others were to be demolished or sold.

Low-rent housing for defense and defense-related workers was authorized under the Lanham Act as a temporary measure[41] to entice defense and defense-related workers to stay on their jobs by offering them special housing incentives.[42] Some Lanham Act housing was permanent, but this consisted of projects started before the war and temporarily transferred to war use. During the war, the basis for eligibility was shifted from household economic need to the nation's need for defense workers. Due to employment discrimination as well as demographics, African-Americans initially comprised a small proportion of defense workers and hence, in 1942, no more than 3 percent were eligible for defense housing.[43] The proportion of African-Americans employed in defense work and living in war housing projects increased in 1943 and 1944 as labor shortages were felt by many industries (see Table 5.12).

In localities with racially mixed war housing, the actual level of racial integration varied substantially from project to project. In six racially integrated housing projects in Cleveland, for example, the actual proportion of African-Americans among tenants in 1945 varied from 0.25 percent (2 of 796 units) at one project, to over 99 percent (all but 8 of 1,267 units) at another (see Table 5.13).

Similar patterns were evident in the integrated housing projects in other cities, with one striking exception.[44] New York City's tenant distribution largely was racially equitable.[45] The more extreme deviations of occupancy (at least two projects were over 75% black, while at least two others were less than 8% black) could be explained to some extent by the *proximity rule* which gave priority in admission to eligible residents of the project's immediate area.[46]

In 1945, there were over one thousand federally subsidized housing projects, containing a total of about 760,000 units, in the United States. Just 746 of these projects, containing fewer than 120,000 units, had African-American tenants; these included 196 all-black and 465 racially bisected projects containing about 48,000 and 59,000 units respectively. Only 85 projects, containing fewer than 13,000 units, were actually racially mixed with no special restrictions on occupancy.[47] This racially restrictive distribution is confirmed by referring to another tabulation carried out by the Federal Public Housing Authority in 1945. As in the 1944 case, between 9 and 10 percent of all hous-

Table 5.12
Share of Blacks in the War Housing Program: Private and Public Accommodations, 1941–1944

Housing Source	1941		1942		1943		1944	
	Total	Black	Total	Black	Total	Black	Total	Black
Private	187,200	553	412,058	1,715	557,617	15,038	573,602	24,945
Public	144,367	4,050	601,678	35,407	781,637	66,637	762,539	90,444
Total	331,567	4,603	1,013,736	37,122	1,339,254	81,675	1,336,141	115,389

Source: National Housing Agency: Race Relations Documents (March 1947).

Table 5.13
Racial Composition of Integrated Projects in
Cleveland, 1945

			Black Units	
Name of Projects	Total Units	White Units	Total	%
Lake Shore Village	796	794	2	0.25
Seville Homes	434	11	423	97.46
Carver Park	1,267	8	1,259	99.37
Cedar Central Apts	640	621	19	2.97
Berea Homes[a]	506	464	36	7.11

[a]Six units in the project were occupied by tenants of Japanese
origin.

ing projects were racially integrated, but the 1945 data show a greater proportion of racially bisected housing projects (see Table 5.14).

Values of the two estimates of the index of racial segregation calculated for
wartime public housing are given in Table 5.15. Overall, the level of racial
segregation in war housing appears to be higher than before the war, with the
lowest level in the West (0.29 and 0.33), and the highest in the Midwest (0.40
and 0.54). These levels were due to two related reasons. First, despite some

Table 5.14
Distribution of Units by Racial Types of
Housing in Housing Projects with Black
Occupancy, 1945

	Total Units		
Racial Types of Projects	Projects	Units	%
All black	196	48,473	41
Racially bisected	77	11,455	10
Partially bisected	388	47,431	40
Racially integrated	85	12,226	10
Total	**746**	**119,585**	**100**

Table 5.15
Estimates of the Index of Racial Segregation in the War Housing
Program, 1944

					Public Housing	
					Estimates (I_n)	
			Black Units		Based on	
Regions	All Units	Total	Total	Percent	First Method	Second Method
Northeast	223,927	115,886	14,060	12.13	0.35	0.42
Midwest	264,504	106,345	14,794	13.91	0.40	0.54
South[a]	342,691	199,829	17,008	8.51	0.38	0.46
West	422,928	266,887	26,605	9.97	0.29	0.33
U.S.	**1,254,050**	**688,947**	**72,467**	**10.52**	**0.32**	**0.43**

Source: National Housing Agency, Federal Public Housing Authority, *Negro Share of Priority War Housing—Private and Public, as of December, 1944*, Report S-602, December 31, 1944.

[a]Southwest and South are combined.

small participation of African-Americans in the war housing program, this group rarely shared the same housing projects with white defense workers. Indeed, in Buffalo, Detroit, San Diego, Baltimore, and other cities, African-Americans were routinely denied vacant units in white projects. As a result, the proportion of racially homogeneous housing projects was relatively large.[48]

Second, racial discrimination in access to units during the war was less subtle and more widespread than before and took place in a context of pervasive employment discrimination, with many jobs, even in labor-short defense industries, "closed to Negroes."[49] According to a 1942 survey of the Bureau of Employment Security,[50] which concentrated on regions with considerable African-American labor, 144,583 of 282,245 prospective openings (51%) were barred to black workers as a matter of policy. The responses to this survey came as wartime labor shortages were becoming significant in many industries and were made to a federal agency about two months after the president had called for the abolition of discrimination in war industries.

Even eligible blacks were often excluded from white housing projects. According to Edwin Embree of the Julius Rosenwald Fund in 1945,

Funds available for housing Negro defense workers in more than twenty-five Northern cities could not be used for over a year because of objection from white residents. In Detroit, where the 150,000 Negroes of the 1940 census have increased by 10 percent every year during the war years, colored tenants could move into public housing built expressly for them only after crashing a picket line of white rioters. In Baltimore, where the numbers have jumped from 165,000 in 1940 to over 200,000 in 1944, an angry citizenry has refused to let Negroes move out of established ghettos or have public housing.[51]

Although the data are sketchy, it appears that federal and local housing authorities were often united in reserving housing projects exclusively for families from only one racial group.[52] Some 3,000 units of subsidized housing in Detroit were vacant but "closed to eligible Negro" defense workers as a matter of policy in 1943.[53] Similar situations existed in Buffalo, Philadelphia, and many other cities.[54]

Racial discrimination in access to war housing did not mean that all white defense workers received subsidized housing. For most PHAs (including areas of priority war housing), a shortage of units was the rule. In Detroit, for example, of 31,100 units approved in 1942 as the minimum requirement, only 8,500 units were actually built.[55]

PATTERNS OF INCOME DISPERSAL IN WAR HOUSING

Incomplete data and summary reports of federal housing agencies indicate that war housing projects tended to be located on vacant sites accessible to transportation and utilities or in close proximity to war plants. Most clearance for the purpose of low-income housing construction was suspended to "conserve critical labor resources and construction materials."[56] Nevertheless, the siting of war housing projects was not significantly different from that of USHA or PWA housing. Moreover, almost all temporary housing built on vacant sites not adjacent to previous low-income residential areas were dismantled at the end of the war.[57]

An estimate of the index of income separation could not be calculated for war housing. The patterns of dispersal of these projects, however, do not appear to be substantially different from early patterns of concentration in low-income areas.

CONCLUSIONS ABOUT WAR HOUSING

In summary, war housing was largely segregated by race, both in access to the program and in assignment to units. Indeed, the level of racial segregation and discrimination in war housing was unprecedented, with African-American housing partially or totally excluded from war housing in most of the Northeast, Midwest, and West—even as earlier patterns continued in the South with the complete separation of the racial groups there.

Although an estimate of the index of income separation was not derived for war housing, the pattern of dispersal of the projects, particularly those intended to continue in use after the war, was not substantially different from that of the earlier programs.

POSTWAR PUBLIC HOUSING, 1946–1963

Except for some designed for returning war veterans (Veterans' Reuse housing), virtually no new construction of public housing was undertaken between 1946 and 1949. Housing authorities were instead directed by Congress to dispose of war housing and remove income-ineligible families from permanent federally supported housing projects. The construction of low-income public housing revived somewhat following the adoption in 1949 of a new housing act. Although relevant data are sketchy, they strongly suggest a continuation of racial segregation and income separation.

PATTERNS OF INCOME DISPERSAL

In 1953, 92 urban renewal projects containing 8,517 subsidized units received final approval from the Urban Renewal Administration,[58] all of them slum-clearance housing in Pennsylvania, Illinois, and Virginia and hence located in the low-income area.[59] By 1960, a total of 322 urban renewal projects in 195 cities with 14,147 units had been completed.[60] Over 80 percent of these units were located in low-income areas,[61] according to data on the relocation of displaced families for the period 1949–1960.[62]

Most housing projects outside low-income areas were built for elderly households, most of them white. In 1960, for example, 68 percent of households moving into elderly housing projects were white.

From our operational definition of income separation, the estimate of the index of income separation (D_n) of low-income housing for the period 1949–1960 is, after substitution, equal to 0.31. The reduction in the level of income separation largely reflects the construction of elderly housing in noncentral-city areas.

PATTERNS OF RACIAL OCCUPANCY

According to the Public Housing Administration, 38 percent of public housing units were occupied by black tenants in 1952 and 47 percent in 1963, a year in which seventeen states in the continental United States had laws prohibiting racial discrimination in publicly assisted housing.[63] Although open racial occupancy did not necessarily mean racial integration, it could create patterns of racial occupancy measurably different from those in jurisdictions which maintained policies of complete racial separation of tenants, including most if not all Southern states during this period (see Table 5.16).[64]

Racial occupancy data for localities with open racial occupancy for the period 1953–1963 were collected by the Race Relations Branch of the Public

Table 5.16
Pattern of Occupancy and Index of Racial Segregation in Low-Rent Public Housing in Three States, 1953–1962

Years	State	Total Program		Total Occupied by Black Tenants in Program						Index
						Integrated Projects		Segregated Projects		
		Projects	Units	Projects	Units	Projects	Units	Projects	Units	
1953	California	180	62,297	132	14,304	78	7,885	0	6,419	0.08
	New Jersey	57	12,904	44	3,161	29	1,696	15	1,465	0.09
	New York	44	17,512	38	8,697	31	8,550	7	147	0.00
1954	California	200	65,380	128	13,083	79	7,434	49	5,649	0.07
	New Jersey	83	20,998	55	4,558	39	3,044	16	1,514	0.06
	New York	69	50,381	48	9,393	43	9,239	5	154	0.00
1955	California	152	44,812	114	13,492	80	11,430	34	2,062	0.03
	New Jersey	81	19,919	61	6,230	44	4,494	17	1,736	0.06
	New York	59	42,800	53	12,380	49	12,238	4	142	0.00
1956	California	108	19,240	73	8,118	60	7,484	13	634	0.02
	New Jersey	77	20,742	60	6,766	41	4,613	19	2,153	0.07
	New York	60	40,084	57	13,981	51	13,506	6	475	0.01

Year	State									
1957	California	114	21,028	81	9,325	72	8,873	9	452	0.01
	New Jersey	82	22,212	64	7,565	46	5,192	18	2,373	0.07
	New York	65	43,813	57	15,722	52	15,248	5	474	0.01
1958	California	114	21,541	78	9,458	67	8,662	11	796	0.02
	New Jersey	82	22,366	65	7,804	46	5,535	19	2,269	0.07
	New York	65	46,795	58	17,667	52	17,192	6	475	0.01
1959	California	125	22,284	87	9,878	78	9,552	9	326	0.01
	New Jersey	97	23,228	78	8,119	59	5,717	19	2,402	0.07
	New York	67	47,825	61	18,450	55	16,575	6	1,875	0.02
1960	California	144	22,984	92	9,993	84	9,683	8	310	0.01
	New Jersey	102	23,936	83	8,534	63	6,020	20	2,514	0.07
	New York	71	50,791	64	18,955	59	18,436	5	519	0.01
1961	California	150	25,329	102	10,485	86	9,887	16	598	0.01
	New Jersey	110	26,095	91	10,197	69	7,680	22	2,517	0.06
	New York	77	51,833	70	19,514	65	18,993	5	521	0.01
1962	California	162	24,445	112	10,894	98	9,963	14	931	0.02
	New Jersey	124	27,276	100	10,681	75	7,899	25	2,782	0.06
	New York	86	55,048	74	21,144	67	20,013	7	1,131	0.01

Housing Administration and published in the *Directory of State and Local Progress Toward Open Occupancy in Low-Rent Projects*, or the *Directory*. While this is the most complete collection of racial occupancy data available, it provides no information on the racial composition of tenants in individual housing projects or the racial composition of waiting lists in individual PHAs.

Moreover, the *Directory* reports racial occupancy data by groups of housing projects known as *management combinations*; in fact, the data are effectively aggregated at the state level. Nevertheless, a modified estimate $I'_{xpha(assign)}$ of the index of racial segregation may be calculated based on these data.

Specifically, the variables $\sum N_j$, $T_{xj(expect)}$, $P_{xj(actual)}$, and $DIFF'_{xj(assign)}$ are determined at the state level rather than the PHA level. Even though this level of aggregation obscures intrastate variations and is far less precise than calculations relative to ideal PHA-level data, some inferences can be drawn.

The derivation of the estimates $I_{xpha(assign)}$ and the relevant *Directory* data, are given in Table 5.16 for California, New York, and New Jersey in various years. As the first line of this table shows, according to the *Directory*, 62,297 units of public housing were occupied in California in 1953, 14,304 of them (23%) by black tenants and the remainder by whites and other racial groups; 7,885 of the 14,304 black-occupied units were in projects classified as completely integrated, and the other 6,419 were in segregated Negro projects. The other lines are interpreted similarly.

Assuming that completely integrated projects were occupied according to the statewide proportions of tenants from different racial groups, the determination of the index can be reduced to the determination of the proportion of units that must be reassigned to arrive at a neutral distribution of blacks in the segregated Negro projects.[65] Using the deviation $DIFF'_b$ of the proportion $P_{b(actual)}$ of black tenants in segregated projects from the proportion $T_{b(expect)}$ among tenants statewide, the estimate $I'_{bxpha(assign)}$ of the index of racial segregation is calculated as:

$$I'_{bstate(assign)} = \frac{DIFF'_{b(assign)} * N_s}{N} \qquad (25)$$

where N_s is the total number of units in segregated Negro projects, N is the total number of units in the state, and $DIFF'_{b(assign)}$ is as described above. The values of this index are given in column 11 of Table 5.16.

New York had the lowest values of the index, reflecting the fact that of the three states, New York had (relatively) the smallest number of units in Negro projects.

The second estimate $I'_{xstate(admit)}$ of the index, based of the shares of racial groups in all (tenant and nontenant) household units in the state, is derived by replacing the racial group's statewide share of public housing tenants by their shares of household units. At the national level, the index is estimated as the weighted average of state indices, with more weight given to states with more units (see Table 5.17).

Table 5.17
Estimates of the Index of Racial Segregation in States with Open Racial Occupancy, 1954–1962

			Estimates (I_n) Based on	
Year	Total Units	Percent Black	First Method	Second Method
1954	242,021	25.89	0.07	0.09
1955	193,096	39.32	0.06	0.08
1956	168,050	48.37	0.07	0.14
1957	181,857	51.29	0.07	0.15
1958	188,890	54.19	0.07	0.14
1959	201,530	53.84	0.07	0.15
1960	210,032	54.63	0.06	0.15
1961	222,115	55.46	0.06	0.15
1962	228,003	56.61	0.06	0.15

Source: Based on data from HHFA, Intergroup Relations Branch, *Trends Toward Open Occupancy in Low-Rent Housing: Progress by the Public Housing Administration* (1955–1963).

These state-level estimates of the index of racial segregation tend to understate the actual levels of racial segregation, since all PHAs in the state are aggregated regardless of individual patterns of racial occupancy. Although the national estimates of the index of racial segregation appear to be generally low, they are fairly high in individual states, notably in the Midwest; 11,119 of the 17,153 units occupied by black tenants in Illinois in 1961, for example, were in segregated Negro projects.[66]

The removal of income-ineligible families played a significant role in explaining this change in the patterns of racial occupancy in the post-war housing program. Since wartime public housing was occupied predominantly by employed white workers, most of the income-ineligible families removed were white families. In 1949 alone, for example, nearly 44,000 families, 74 percent of which were white, were deemed ineligible for continued occupancy on the basis of income.

Data on admission and continued occupancy show that more than 71 percent of "Negro and other" households but only 52 percent of whites admitted in 1955 were still eligible for assistance a year later. This was both a short- and long-term trend. Twenty-two percent of the "Negro and other" households but only 5 percent of the white households admitted in 1944 remained eligible for assistance twelve years later, in 1956.[67]

Having examined the qualitatively different portions of public housing in the post-war period, we now merge these measures to obtain the best aggregate measure of racial segregation for the period (see Table 5.18). The values of both estimates are substantially below wartime levels.

SUMMARY: PATTERNS OF SEGREGATION IN THE EARLY PERIOD

The analysis of patterns of racial occupancy and income dispersal of subsidized low-rent housing shows persistent and pervasive racial segregation and income separation in federally subsidized housing during the period 1932–1963. This is reflected in the estimates of the indices of racial and income separation.

In the experimental program of the Housing Division of the PWA, the separation of tenants by race was nearly uniform and complete. Housing projects

Table 5.18
Estimates of the Index of Racial Segregation in Low-Rent Public Housing, 1954–1962

Year	Total Units	Units in States with Occupancy Pattern		Estimates (I_n) Based on	
		Open	Segregated	Assign	Admit
1954	309,578	242,021	67,557	0.21	0.38
1955	252,900	193,096	59,804	0.20	0.37
1956	208,576	168,050	40,526	0.18	0.29
1957	230,522	181,857	48,665	0.19	0.31
1958	241,943	188,890	53,053	0.19	0.36
1959	250,379	201,530	48,849	0.18	0.35
1960	261,093	210,032	51,061	0.18	0.33
1961	275,904	222,115	53,789	0.17	0.30
1962	291,086	228,003	63,083	0.19	0.29

Source: Based on data from HHFA, Intergroup Relations Branch, *Trends Toward Open Occupancy in Low-Rent Housing: Progress by the Public Housing Administration* (1955–1963).

were frequently designated for tenants from only one race from initial planning, and some planned as multiracial were operated for only one race. Over half of the mixed projects were in fact segregated by building or wing. This continued under the USHA, although the degree of participation of minority racial groups in their program was substantially higher than previously.

In addition to the separation of tenants by race, the overall allocations of units appears to have been racially discriminatory. Although African-Americans comprised the majority of applicants eligible for public housing assistance, whites received the largest total share of units in the public housing program. Overall, whites as a group received nearly 6 percent more units than their proportion among all applicants eligible for public housing assistance would have justified.

During World War II, racial segregation in public housing intensified. As the value of the index indicates, the level of racial separation in the war housing program was the highest since the inception of the low-rent housing. Federal housing policy condoned exclusion of blacks from war housing projects.

After World War II, the level of racial segregation of tenants in subsidized housing declined steadily as many states and localities began to adopt laws and administrative directives prohibiting racial segregation and discrimination in public housing. However, this reduction in the level of racial segregation occurred in the context of a rapid removal of income-ineligible tenants, the majority of whom were white, and public housing in many communities (in the North and South) increasingly took on the appearance of Negro housing. This trend was further reinforced by the introduction of alternative housing subsidy programs, especially for the elderly. African-Americans, who were once denied access to vacant units in family housing projects, quickly became the primary clients of that program after World War II.

Subsidized housing was also very separated by income. Under the PWA, housing projects were located exclusively in low-income areas, strongly suggesting that the public housing programs were more instruments of central-city reorganization, receptables for displaced low-income families, than welfare programs for the poor. Under the USHA, housing projects continued to be economically isolated. The central criteria in the selection of sites for housing projects were land cost and design and construction for economy, so that "slum" and vacant sites were the preferred locations for housing projects. From the end of the war through 1963, public housing projects continued to be located primarily in low-income areas, but public housing began to be built outside the central city as suburban communities in search of renewal and redevelopment funds from the URA were forced to accept some low-income housing. This improved the patterns of income dispersal, based on the assumption that all housing projects built in noncentral-city areas were located in the moderate-high-income area, although the suburbanization of low-income housing may not in fact have substantially reduced the economic isolation of the tenants.

NOTES

1. In addition to 51 housing projects, the Housing Division also financed seven limited dividend housing projects. Limited dividend housing projects are not included in the analysis.

2. See, for example, Richard Sterner, *The Negro's Share: A Study of Income, Consumption, Housing and Public Assistance*, (New York: Harper and Brothers, 1943), 317. Housing projects in the U.S. Virgin Islands and Puerto Rico are excluded from the analysis.

3. The number of units for which racial occupancy data were available is slightly lower than the total number of units. Racially bisected projects were housing projects divided into two separate living quarters, one exclusively for white tenants and the other exclusively for black tenants.

4. According to the housing manager, "Tenants shall only be selected from applicants found to be eligible in accordance with the standard of eligibility. Only those applicants who are most worthy as shown by our investigation will be chosen. First consideration will be given to those having the highest score as to need for housing, general desirability, and financial surety. In the event of two applicants of equal need, preference will be given to the one who registered first. No other factors may be given consideration and no exception can be made to the above rules." Public Housing Administration, Records of the Housing Division of PWA, 1933–1937, statement by Charles J. McMenimen, Housing Manager, RG 196, Project H–8501, New Towne Court (September 20, 1937), National Archives.

5. Public Housing Administration, Records of the Housing Division of PWA, 1933–1937, RG 196, Project H–1001, Cedar Central Apartments, Cleveland, Ohio, National Archives.

6. Public Housing Administration, Records of the Housing Division of PWA, 1933–1937, RG 196, Project H–9001, Wayne, PA (1937), National Archives; see also Elizabeth Longan, "Progress by Local and State Agencies," *Housing Yearbook* (1938): 40–117 passim.

7. Public Housing Administration, Records of the Housing Division of PWA, 1933–1937, RG 196, Project H–20001, Omaha, Nebraska, National Archives.

8. Public Housing Administration, Records of the Housing Division of PWA, 1933–1937, RG 196, Project H–1502, Milwaukee, Wisconsin, National Archives.

9. Recall that the index is calculated by subtracting the proportion of blacks (whites) among all tenants in each housing project from the PHA-wide proportion of black (white) tenants to obtain the deviation DIFF. Since the index assumes that the racial composition of tenants in the PHA is the standard of unsegregated occupancy, the deviation is equal to zero if blacks (whites) as a group are represented in all housing projects as in the PHA as a whole, and different from zero when blacks (whites) as a group are not represented in housing projects as in the PHA as a whole. By multiplying the deviation by the total number of units in housing project j, we find the number of units in project j that would have to be redistributed to arrive at a racially neutral assignment of tenants in j. Adding the number for tenants to be redistributed for all housing projects give us the number of blacks (whites) that must be reassigned to achieve a racially neutral distribution of tenants within the PHA.

10. The table indicates a substantial variation across PHAs. For some housing projects like the Outhwaite Homes in Cleveland, Parklawn in Milwaukee, College

Court in Louisville, Lauderdale Courts in Memphis, Harlem River Houses in New York City, and Riverside Heights in Montgomery, Alabama, the deviation indicates a greater disproportion between the racial composition of tenants in those projects and their corresponding PHA-wide racial composition of tenants than in other projects.

11. Nearly 99 of every 100 families eligible for public housing could not be accommodated by the Housing Division's program. "So far as I have been able to visit occupied Housing Division projects, I have found the tenants bona fide working-class families who had previously lived in antiquated housing. They had been carefully chosen from a great number of other deserving applicants and were radiantly happy in their new surroundings. It is hard to see what social purpose would be served by evicting them to make room for another set of working-class families whose annual incomes are a hundred or so dollars less. More than 99 of every 100 eligible families have to wait their turn in either case." Edith Elmer Wood, "Rents in PWA Housing Division Projects," *Public Housing Progress* (June 1937): 4.

12. "Being Negroes as well as the most recently arrived labor group, they were marked for industrial decimation. . . . When after the lean years (and there were more than seven of them) prosperity came back, it pointedly avoided the colored unemployed." "The Negro's War," *Fortune* (June 1942): 78.

13. The four projects were Highland Homes in Wayne, Pennsylvania; Schonowee Village in Schenectady, New York; Westfield Acres in Camden, New Jersey; and Lincoln Gardens in Evansville, Indiana. Lincoln Gardens, an all-black housing project in Evansville, Indiana, was located in an industrial district primarily to provide "labor for Chrysler Corporation and the Graham–Paige Body plant by the Briggs Body Manufacturing Company." Public Housing Administration, Records of the Housing Division of PWA, 1933–1937, RG 196, Box 270; see also Public Housing Administration, Records of the Housing Division of PWA, 1933–1937, RG 196, "Application of Capitol Planning and Housing Corporation Atlanta, Georgia, November 23, 1933," National Archives.

14. See U.S. Housing and Home Finance Agency, Public Housing Administration, *Low-Rent Public Housing, Planning, Design, and Construction for Economy* (Washington, D.C.: Housing and Home Finance Agency, December 1950).

15. Robert C. Weaver, "Racial Minorities and Public Housing," in *Proceedings of the National Conference of Social Work* (New York: Columbia University Press, 1940).

16. "Tenant Policy Threatens Housing Program," *Public Housing Progress* (April 15, 1935).

17. Public Housing Administration, "Application of Capitol Planning," RG 196.

18. Determining the number of housing projects (units) built by the USHA is not transparent. In June 1941, it was reported that 213 housing projects were "being tenanted." This number included housing projects transferred before completion to the War and Navy Department. According to some estimates, the program of the USHA consisted of "139,000 dwelling units . . . located in 380 different projects." Sterner, *The Negro's Share*, 320.

19. "In most of the cases in which both Negroes and whites live in the same projects, they are segregated in different wings. There are a few cases, however, particularly in New York City, in which Negroes and whites live together without any kind of segregation. In spite of this, the USHA housing projects have, on the whole, strengthened rather than weakened housing segregation." Sterner, *The Negro's Share*, 320.

20. Units in some housing projects were occupied by enlisted personnel of the U.S.

Army. In Jacksonville, Florida, 60 units at Brentwood Park were occupied by enlisted personnel of the Army. In Charlotte, North Carolina, 60 units at Piedmont Courts were occupied by enlisted personnel of the Army, as were 50 units at Bayview Homes in Biloxi, Mississippi; 100 units in Gonzales Gardens in Columbia, South Carolina; and 30 percent of units at Tays Place in El Paso, Texas.

21. According to the 1941 Annual Report of the New York City Housing Authority, the nativity of tenants in public housing projects "in general corresponds to that of New York City population as a whole." Overall, 88 percent of tenants were white, 12 percent were African-American, and less than 1 percent were from other racial groups. The Authority, however, gave no racial breakdown of the eleven individual housing projects. See New York City Housing Authority, *Eighth Annual Report* (New York: New York City Housing Authority, 1941), 10–23 passim.

22. See Housing Authority of the City of Charlotte, North Carolina, *Annual Report,* (Charlotte: Housing Authority of the City of Charlotte, 1942).

23. The term *tenant* refers to the household unit in a housing project, not to an individual person.

24. Note that since there are only two racial groups of tenants in the PHA, the estimate I_{xpha} will be the same for both racial groups of tenants.

25. The number of units have been rounded.

26. The projects were Queensbridge Houses, Red Hook Houses, and Vladeck Houses.

27. The racial composition of two PWA projects in New York City (Harlem River Houses and Williamsburg Houses) was not reported in 1941.

28. In part, racial discrimination in access to units was reinforced by the system of a separate waiting list for each housing project. Eligibility rules varied among PHAs. To be eligible for public housing in New York City, for example, an applicant had to demonstrate among other things that his current unit was substandard; that he resided in this substandard unit for more than one year; that he was a New York City resident for more than two years and his income was within the admission limit; that he had a family; and that he was a U.S. citizen. Of all applications submitted to the New York City Housing Authority in 1941, only 20 percent of households met these eligibility requirements. See New York City Housing Authority, *Eighth Annual Report*, 10–11.

29. In general, there can be considerable time lags between the filing of an application and the actual assignment of the household to a unit. Since the date of the initial filing of applications was not reported, we assumed that the list of applicants represents a cumulative list through 1941.

30. Sterner, *The Negro's Share*, 320.

31. According to the administrator of the Federal Public Housing Authority, John Blandford, "racial restrictive covenants, as the core of a system of traditional real estate practices controlling the access of Negroes and other minority groups to sites and dwellings units, have affected practically every phase of public housing administration during the past thirteen years. By generally restricting these groups to sharply defined neighborhoods which provide too few houses and too little living space, these covenants have served to distort the objectives of the public housing program. The ultimate effect of covenanted land restrictions is to place the Federal agency, required as it is to clear and replace slum areas, in the position of appearing to place the stamp of governmental approval upon separate residential patterns and to render it most difficult for the agency to administer public funds in such manner as to assure equitable

participation by racial groups." John B. Blandford, Jr., "The Need for Low-Cost Housing," speech delivered at the Annual Conference of the National Urban League, Columbus, Ohio, 2 October 1944, quoted in Robert C. Weaver, *The Negro Ghetto* (New York: Russell & Russell, 1948), 176.

32. B. J. Hovde, "Negro Housing in Pittsburgh," *Opportunity* (December 1938): 356–358.

33. According to Myrdal, the "Negro has received a large share of the benefits under this [USHA] program. Indeed, the USHA has given him a better deal than has any other major federal public welfare agency. This may be due, in part, to the fact that, so far, subsidized housing projects have been built in urban areas, where, even in the South, there is less reluctance to consider the Negro's needs. The main explanation, however, is just the fact that the USHA has had the definite policy of giving the Negro his share. It has a special division for nonwhite races, headed by a Negro who can serve as spokesman for his people. Many of the leading white officials of the agency, as well, are known to have been convinced in principle that discrimination should be actively fought." Gunnar Karl Myrdal, *An American Dilemma* (New York: Harper & Brothers, 1944), 350.

34. See, for example, Elizabeth Wood, "Tenant Selection in a Locally Operated Project," in *Managing Low-Rent Housing: A Record of Current Experience and Practice in Public Housing* (Chicago: National Association of Housing Officials, March 1939).

35. The difference between the number of projects reported here and the number of projects completely or 95 percent occupied is the number of projects placed under construction.

36. "In selecting sites under the pre-war USHA program," wrote Booker T. McGraw, "when Negro occupancy was involved, the general practice was to clear a slum neighborhood predominantly or totally occupied by Negroes. The project erected on this site was then occupied predominantly or totally by Negroes. This same procedure was followed in providing homes for white occupancy. In some instances areas occupied by Negroes or by Negroes and others were cleared, but each project provided was restricted to a single racial group. This occurred in spite of the site selection policy which stated that areas occupied by minority racial groups were in general to be utilized for the development of projects to which these groups would be admitted. This policy further indicated that when areas occupied by more than one group were cleared for development the resulting projects were to be open to the same racial groups who formerly occupied the site . . . the local practices, generally supported by federal policy and procedure, was to locate . . . projects upon sites which would duplicate or at least not disturb the prevalent neighborhood pattern. The difficulty arises in the wide latitude of the definition of neighborhood pattern." Booker T. McGraw, "Report of Field Trip—Region VI," RG 196, National Archives.

37. See National Housing Conference, *Public Housing Tour Guide* (New York: National Housing Conference, 1940).

38. Ibid.; see also A. Bickford and Douglas S. Massey, "Segregation in the Second Ghetto: Racial and Ethnic Segregation in American Public Housing, 1977," *Social Forces* 69, 4 (June 1991): 1012–1013.

39. Assuming an equal division of the PHA between the low- and moderate-high-income areas.

40. See U.S. Housing and Home Finance Agency, *Low-Rent Public Housing, Planning, Design, and Construction for Economy* (Washington, D.C.: Housing and Home

Finance Agency, December 1950); see also Clarence W. Beatty, "Urban Redevelopment—What Is the Value of Vacant Land in Blighted Areas?" *Journal of Housing* (January 1947): 8–9.

41. Herbert Emmerich, "Public Housing in 1943," *Housing Yearbook* (1944): 27–46.

42. The level of federal rent subsidies in defense housing projects was actually quite low. "Although they [the tenants] are probably paying a smaller proportion of income for rent than they would if they were selecting from an unlimited market, they are paying what the FPHA housing accommodations are worth." In 1943, for example, rents in 98 percent of war housing projects "varied only from an average of $31.65 per month for the lowest income group to $33.99 for the highest, a narrow range which reflects FPHA's policy to build dwellings of a more or less uniform character and to set rents based on the market." See "FPHA Rents," *FPHA Bulletin* 52 (September 1943): 3.

43. National Housing Agency, Office of the Administrator, *Negro Share of Priority War Housing—Private and Public as of December 31, 1944* (Washington, D.C.: National Housing Agency, 1 May 1945), Table 5; see also National Housing Agency, Office of the Administrator, "Housing Negroes and Other Minority Group War Workers in Region IX: A Memorandum from Robert Taylor, NHA and Frank Horne, FPHA," dated 21 November 1942, RG 196, National Archives.

44. The proportion of blacks in individual housing projects in the Los Angeles PHA varied from 0.5 percent to 97.5 percent. See, for example, Weaver, *The Negro Ghetto*, 191.

45. In Springfield, Illinois, in the John Hay Homes housing project, 499 out of 599 units were occupied in 1942. Approximately 100 units (or 20% of the total) were occupied by black tenants. There was "no section reserved for Negroes and correspondingly none for whites. Apartments have been let solely on the size of the individual family and the unit which were available." See William M. Asby, "No Jim Crow in Springfield Federal Housing," *Opportunity* (June 1942): 170.

46. According to the chairman of the Housing Authority, in selecting tenants priority was given to former site residents and veterans. Then "to assure equal treatment: preliminary registrations on which there is no information about race, are filed by mail. The information is translated into code numbers and the name into a serial number. . . . Families are called for interviews as they are sorted by machines, according to their need and priority." Thomas F. Farrell, "Object Lesson in Race Relations," *New York Times Magazine*, 12 February 1950; see also "Racial Friction is Found Absent in Housing Unit," *Herald Tribune* (New York) 5 January 1946, 22; Edmund B. Butler, "Race Relations and Public Housing," *Interracial Review* (March 1947): 38–40. For a list of other localities with racially integrated public housing projects, see "Gains Made in Housing To Improve Racial Amity," *Philadelphia Record*, 26 February 1946, 11.

47. Weaver, *The Negro Ghetto*, 180.

48. Race riots broke out early during the war in Detroit and Buffalo when black defense workers attempted to move into housing projects previously occupied only by white workers. According to *Fortune*, the "story of the Sojourner Truth project in Detroit has become a cause célèbre with repercussions high in the federal bureaucracy. The riot hit not only bystanders in Detroit's streets but also the Director of Defense Housing in FWA [Federal Work Administration], Clark Foreman. This scion of a leading southern family lost his job, under some congressional pressure, because he supported too firmly the Negroes' insistence on their rights. But more revealing than the skirmish of Detroit, because more typical, is the stalemate of Buffalo." See "The Negro's War," *Fortune* (June 1942): 80. Other PHAs with vacant units denied to

black defense workers include Kingsbury–La Porte in Indiana, Ravenna in Ohio, Bradford in Virginia, and Pt. Pleasant in West Virginia. See "Housing Awaits Workers in Some Localities," *FPHA Bulletin* 51 (September 1943): 3.

49. *Fortune*, June 1942, 79.

50. Black workers were generally imported by northern industries to be used as stand-by laborers. National Housing Agency, Federal Public Housing Authority, Statistics Division, *Families in Low-Rent Housing: Data on Income, Rent, and Number of Persons in Families Reexamined for Continued Occupancy in Projects Constructed Under PL–412 and in PWA Projects January–June, 1944*, Report S-550 (Washington, D.C.: National Housing Agency, 1944), Table 8; U.S. Housing and Home Finance Agency, Public Housing Administration, *Families in Low-Rent Projects Reexamined for Continued Occupancy during Calendar Year 1956*, Report 225.1 (Washington, D.C.: Housing and Home Finance Agency, October 1957); Housing and Home Finance Agency, *Families Moving into Low-Rent Housing*, Report 226.1 (Washington, D.C.: Housing and Home Finance Agency, September 1957), 2–23 passim.

51. Edwin R. Embree, "Balance Sheet in Race Relations," *The Atlantic Monthly* 175, 5 (May 1945): 88.

52. See, for example, McGraw, "The Provision of Housing," 11. For an extended discussion of the race problem in low-rent housing in the Northeast region see William L. Evans, *Race Fear and Housing in a Typical American Community* (New York: National Urban League, 1946), 9–35 passim; Herman H. Long and Charles S. Johnson, *People v. Property: Race Restrictive Covenants in Housing* (Nashville: Fisk University Press, 1947); Charles S. Johnson, *To Stem this Tide: A Survey of Racial Tension Areas in the United States* (New York: Pilgrim Press, 1943).

53. As the result of intense protests by black defense workers themselves, the Commissioner of the FPHA ordered the construction of additional units for black defense workers in the Detroit area. See "More Housing to Help Meet Needs of Detroit Negroes," *FPHA Bulletin* 2, 3 (1944): 3; "The Lesson of Willow Run," *Task* (15 October 1943): 9–18.

54. For an extended discussion, see Evans, *Race Fear and Housing,* 9–35 passim; according to the Commissioner of FPHA, the reason for the vacancies in war housing was that "war housing was being held at the request of specific war industries to accommodate possible future needs, much as certain types of war plants are held as standbys. . . . In addition to reserves, some vacancies are inevitable because of revisions in war production schedules caused by revised battlefront demands; elimination of some production items, causing complete shutdowns and shifts of workers; improved production methods; and retarded recruitment drives," Emmerich, "Public Housing in 1943," 35; see also Weaver, *The Negro Ghetto*, 167; McGraw, "Report of Field Trip—Region VI," RG 196, National Archives.

55. See "The Lesson of Willow Run," *Task* (15 October 1943): 9–17.

56. See National Housing Agency, Office of the Administrator, *Negro Share of Priority War Housing*.

57. Executive Office of the President, Memorandum from the Advisory Commission to the Council of National Defense to Charles Palmer, Defense Housing Coordination, 27 August 1940, RG 196, "War Housing Program," National Archives. See also Weaver, *The Negro Ghetto,* 164–177.

58. See U.S. Housing and Home Finance Agency, Urban Renewal Administration, *Urban Renewal Project Characteristics* (Washington, D.C.: U.S. Housing and Home Finance Agency, September 1955).

59. Ibid. These localities were predominantly suburban.

60. See Harry W. Reynolds, "Population Displacement in Urban Renewal," *The American Journal of Economics and Sociology* 22, 1 (1963): 118–119. Since data on the distribution of housing projects under other housing acts (such as the 1956, elderly, and the 1959, Section 202, housing acts) were not reported separately, we assume that the total number of units include elderly and Section 202 units.

61. Lyle E. Schaller, "Urban Renewal: A Moral Challenge," *The Christian Century* (27 January 1962): 805; "Slum Clearance Pays Extra Dividends," *Reader's Digest* (November 1955); Gerald W. Johnson, "Baltimore Might Make It," *The New Republic* (April 1966):17–18.

62. See U.S. Housing and Home Finance Agency, *Relocation from Urban Renewal Project Areas* (Washington, D.C.: U.S. Housing and Home Finance Agency, 1960), 7.

63. Harry W. Reynolds, "Population Displacement in Urban Renewal," *American Journal of Economics and Sociology* 22, 1 (1963): 118–119; U.S. Housing and Home Finance Agency, Office of the Administrator, Division of Slum Clearance and Urban Redevelopment, *Relocation of Families, Continental United States, through March 1954* (Washington, D.C.: U.S. Housing and Home Finance Agency, 1954); U.S. Housing and Home Finance Agency, Office of the Administrator, Division of Slum Clearance and Urban Redevelopment, *Relocation of Families, Continental United States, through September 1955* (Washington, D.C.: U.S. Housing and Home Finance Agency, Urban Redevelopment Administration, 1955); U.S. Housing and Home Finance Agency, Office of the Administrator, Division of Slum Clearance and Urban Redevelopment, *Summary of Local Redevelopment Programs* (Washington, D.C.: U.S. Housing and Home Finance Agency, Urban Redevelopment Administration, 1952).

64. *Open Racial Occupancy* PHAs are PHAs with a formal commitment to end racial segregation and discrimination in subsidized housing. Units in localities with open racial occupancy are reported in Public Housing Administration, *Directory of State and Local Progress Toward Open Occupancy in Low-Rent Projects* (Washington, D.C.: U. S. Public Housing Administration, 1946–1963), passim. Following New York were Massachusetts (1948), Connecticut, Pennsylvania, and Wisconsin (1949), New Jersey (1950), Rhode Island and Michigan (1952), Minnesota (1955), Oregon (1957), California and Colorado (1959), Indiana (where the principle of nondiscrimination in publicly assisted housing was partially adopted as the result of unfavorable court decisions) and New Hampshire (1961), and Alaska (1962). In Illinois and Ohio, nondiscriminatory provisions were adopted by individual localities and PHAs such as Chicago, Cleveland, and Toledo. In the South, Texas and Louisiana were the only two states to adopt the concept of open racial occupancy in 1956.

65. Assuming that completely integrated projects were racially neutral in occupancy, the integration of white tenants in a state housing program can be reduced to the reassignment of units in segregated white projects according to the statewide racial composition of tenants.

66. The projects were Blue Valley all white, Kessler Road all white, Penn Valley all white, Hospital Hill all white, 43rd and Brooklyn all white, 43rd and Cleveland all white, 20th and Prospect all black, Holmes Square all black, and The Parade all black.

67. U.S. Housing and Home Finance Agency, *Statistics on PHA Operations: Families in Low-Rent Projects* (October 1957). See also idem, *Annual Report* (Washington, D.C.: U.S. Housing and Home Finance Agency, 1950), 327–329; idem, *Occupancy by Negroes Families in Low-Rent Housing by State as of December 31, 1963* (Washington, D.C.: U.S. Housing and Home Finance Agency, 1963), Table 2a.

6

Patterns of Racial Segregation and Economic Isolation, 1964–1992

The presidential Executive Order of 1962, the Civil Rights Act of 1964, and the Fair Housing Act of 1968 in principle banned racial discrimination and segregation in housing programs receiving direct or indirect federal financial assistance.[1] Similarly, the Housing and Community Development Act enacted in 1974 by Congress required federal and local housing authorities to avoid concentrating subsidized housing projects in low-income areas. Thus, racial occupancy patterns and policies of earlier periods were recognized as inequitable and deserving of remedy. Did these patterns in fact change?

PATTERNS OF RACIAL OCCUPANCY IN 1977

Comprehensive and reliable racial occupancy data for subsidized low-rent housing are available only for 1977 and 1992, from surveys of PHAs conducted by the Department of Housing and Urban Development (HUD).[2] Additional data on the racial composition of low-income housing projects were collected by the American Housing Survey. These surveys report data, collected from forms submitted by local housing authorities to HUD, on the numbers of subsidized housing units occupied by families of the various racial and ethnic categories used (these detailed surveys used more disaggregated racial categories than prior efforts, including "White," "Negro/black," "American Indian," "Spanish American," "Oriental," and "Other").[3] Unfortunately, all these data are reported only at the PHA level and not for individual multifamily buildings or projects, placing some limits on the use of the indices of the previous chapters.[4]

The subsidized low-income housing program in the United States in 1977 comprised 1,154,221 units in 9,903 housing projects located in 3,398 PHAs,[5] of which 55,982 units in 278 housing projects were located in Puerto Rico and other U.S. territories, and 14,184 units were in 405 housing projects administered by the Bureau of Indian Affairs in nine states.[6]

In addition to traditional public housing, the 1977 survey covered virtually all federally subsidized low-income housing, most notably the housing for elderly tenants first authorized in 1956 and the Section 8 housing assistance programs.[7] Some units were in more than one housing program. In 1968, for example, the Section 221 (d)(3) BMIR was phased out as a result of excessive mortgage defaults, and units initially authorized under that program were transferred to the Rent Supplement program. In 1974, these units (along with most other multifamily rental programs) were consolidated into the Section 8 housing assistance program.[8]

The analysis here proceeds with a broad classification of housing projects into "Elderly," "Family," and "Mixed Elderly/Family,"[9] because there was a substantial concentration of racial minorities in family housing projects and of whites in elderly housing projects. In 1977, over half of the tenant households in each minority group were in family housing projects: 71 percent of blacks (370,731 of the 523,725 units occupied by blacks); 65 percent of Hispanics; and 55 percent of Asians (see Table 6.1).

Overall, of 4,567 family housing projects 1,193 (26%) were occupied exclusively by racial minorities with no white tenants, and 1,064 additional family housing projects (23%) had ten or fewer white families each (often only one such family). At the same time, in 1977, elderly housing projects were predominantly occupied by white tenants. 151,816 of 188,152 units in elderly housing projects (81% of the total) were occupied by white tenants; 923 elderly housing projects had no black tenants at all, and 601 more had ten or fewer black tenant families each (again often only one).

Data from surveys of tenants in the Section 8, Rent Supplement, and Section 236 programs, though incomplete, indicate continuing patterns of disproportionate concentration of whites in elderly projects and of blacks and other racial minorities in family projects. A 1987 frequency distribution of household heads by race and age shows that at that time, among these tenants, nearly one-third of white household heads but only 9 percent of black household heads were over sixty years of age.

The concentration of tenants by racial group in different subsidy programs is more pronounced at the regional than the national level, partly because of regional disparities in the concentration of different subsidy programs (e.g., the Midwest alone had 40% of all elderly units). The regional distribution of racial groups in low-income housing was quite uneven for this reason and others (see Table 6.2).

Table 6.1
Racial Occupancy of Subsidized Low-Income Housing by Groups of Projects, 1977

Groups of Housing Projects	Total	% of Total	Racial Characteristics of Tenants						
			White	%	Black	%	Hispanic	%	Asian	%
Unknown Group	57,771	5.33	27,747	6.15	23,148	4.42	4,568	5.50	304	4.91
Occupied by Elderly	188,152	17.36	151,816	33.63	26,985	5.15	4,535	5.46	1,087	17.56
Occupied by Family	590,471	54.47	156,882	34.75	370,731	70.79	54,008	65.01	3,415	55.18
Mixed Elderly/Family	247,661	22.85	115,015	25.48	102,861	19.64	19,969	24.04	1,383	22.35
Total	**1,084,055**	**100.00**	**451,460**	**100.00**	**523,725**	**100.00**	**83,080**	**100.00**	**6,189**	**100.00**

Source: U.S. Department of Housing and Urban Development.

Table 6.2
Distribution of All Low-Rent Housing by Census Region

Regions	Total	%	White	%	Black	%	Hispanics	%	Asian	%
Total All Units										
Northeast	354,972	32.74	152,511	33.78	164,113	31.34	36,221	43.60	707	11.42
Midwest	261,318	24.11	132,952	29.45	115,162	21.99	2,185	2.63	288	4.65
South	358,540	33.07	117,065	25.93	216,641	41.37	21,030	25.31	506	8.18
West	109,225	10.08	48,932	10.84	27,809	5.31	23,644	28.46	4,688	75.75
Total	1,084,055	100.00	451,460	100.00	523,725	100.00	83,080	100.00	6,189	100.00
Occupied by Elderly Tenants										
Northeast	64,679	34.38	55,611	36.63	8,406	31.15	499	11.00	47	4.32
Midwest	76,045	40.42	63,203	41.63	10,495	38.89	215	4.74	69	6.35
South	33,107	17.60	21,292	14.02	7,237	26.82	3,144	69.33	10	0.92
West	14,321	7.61	11,710	7.71	847	3.14	677	14.93	961	88.41
Total	188,152	100.00	151,816	100.00	26,985	100.00	4,535	100.00	1,087	100.00

Table 6.2 (*continued*)

Regions	Total	%	White	%	Black	%	Hispanics	%	Asian	%
Occupied by Family Tenants										
Northeast	203,944	34.54	61,905	39.46	116,216	31.35	24,434	45.24	428	12.53
Midwest	109,958	18.62	27,863	17.76	80,093	21.60	1,075	1.99	125	3.66
South	227,244	38.49	53,477	34.09	158,156	42.66	14,584	27.00	435	12.74
West	49,325	8.35	13,637	8.69	16,266	4.39	13,915	25.76	2,427	71.07
Total	**590,471**	**100.00**	**156,882**	**100.00**	**370,731**	**100.00**	**54,008**	**100.00**	**3,415**	**100.00**
Occupied by Family and Elderly Tenants										
Northeast	69,572	28.09	25,319	22.01	32,896	31.98	10,847	54.32	204	14.75
Midwest	63,677	25.71	34,626	30.11	20,918	20.34	417	2.09	84	6.07
South	79,448	32.08	36,481	31.72	40,569	39.44	2,345	11.74	46	3.33
West	34,964	14.12	18,589	16.16	8,478	8.24	6,360	31.85	1,049	75.85
Total	**247,661**	**100.00**	**115,015**	**100.00**	**102,861**	**100.00**	**19,969**	**100.00**	**1,383**	**100.00**

In 1977, over 62 percent of white-occupied units were located in the Midwest and Northeast, the two regions of greatest concentration of elderly housing at that time. Meanwhile, in the South family housing and black tenants predominated; over 41 percent of all black-occupied units were in housing projects located there. Hispanic tenants were most common in the Northeast (which had nearly 44% of Hispanic-occupied units), followed by the West (over 28%) and the South (25%). Most Asian tenants were in the West, which had over 75 percent of all units occupied by Asians.

We derive the estimate $I'_{xpha(assign)}$ of the index of racial segregation, which measures the assignment of racial groups of tenants among housing projects in a PHA, in detail for the elderly housing projects in New Haven, Chicago, and Washington, D.C., in 1977. In that year, New Haven's elderly housing comprised 642 units in ten projects; Chicago's, 4,797 units in twenty-five projects; and Washington's, 1,298 units in eight projects. The racial composition of tenants in the three PHAs varied markedly: 69 percent of New Haven's elderly tenants were white and 30 percent black, while Chicago's were 55 and 44 percent, and Washington's 6 and 93 percent, respectively. Tables 6.3, 6.4, and 6.5 show the proportions $T_{xj(expect)}$ and $P_{xj(actual)}$ and the deviations $DIFF'_{xj(assign)}$ for the three PHAs.

From the deviations $DIFF'_{xj}$ and the total number of units in individual housing projects, the estimate $I_{wpha(assign)}$ of the index of racial segregation for white tenants in Chicago is

$$I'_{wpha(assign)} = \frac{1866}{4797} = 0.39 \tag{26}$$

The corresponding value for black tenants is

$$I'_{bpha(assign)} = \frac{1875}{4797} = 0.39 \tag{27}$$

As Table 6.3 indicates, whites as a group were overrepresented in most elderly housing projects of Chicago relative to their PHA-wide proportion. Similar estimates of the index of racial segregation of tenants for New Haven and Washington are shown in Tables 6.4 and 6.5. Of the three PHAs, the estimate is lowest for Washington, which, however, had very few tenants from any racial group other than black. The estimate is highest for Chicago, where nine of twenty-five housing projects were all black although blacks comprised only 44 percent of elderly tenants. By contrast, in New Haven no elderly housing project was occupied exclusively by one racial group in 1977.

The estimate $I'_{xpha(admit)}$ of the index of racial segregation, which compares the proportion of each racial group among all households, tenants and nontenants, in the PHA with the proportion of the group in individual hous-

Table 6.3
First Estimates of the Index of Racial Segregation in Elderly Housing in Chicago, 1977

Housing Projects	Total Units (N)	Occupied by White Tenants					Occupied by Black Tenants			
		Total	T_w	P_{wj}	DIFF'$_{wj}$	DIFF'$_{wj}$*N	T_b	P_{bj}	DIFF'$_{bj}$	DIFF'$_{bj}$*N
A_1	136	106	0.55	0.78	0.23	31	0.44	0.15	0.29	39
A_2	117	114	0.55	0.97	0.42	49	0.44	0.03	0.41	48
A_3	201	196	0.55	0.98	0.42	85	0.44	0.02	0.41	83
A_4	181	161	0.55	0.89	0.34	61	0.44	0.09	0.34	62
A_5	129	0	0.55	0.00	0.55	71	0.44	1.00	0.56	73
A_6	198	67	0.55	0.34	0.21	43	0.44	0.66	0.22	44
A_7	308	149	0.55	0.48	0.07	21	0.44	0.46	0.03	9
A_8	204	0	0.55	0.00	0.55	113	0.44	1.00	0.56	115
A_9	173	170	0.55	0.98	0.43	74	0.44	0.02	0.42	73
A_{10}	125	0	0.55	0.00	0.55	69	0.44	1.00	0.56	70
A_{11}	137	88	0.55	0.64	0.09	12	0.44	0.35	0.09	12
A_{12}	165	0	0.55	0.00	0.55	91	0.44	1.00	0.56	93
A_{13}	193	0	0.55	0.00	0.55	107	0.44	1.00	0.56	109
A_{14}	154	0	0.55	0.00	0.55	85	0.44	1.00	0.56	87
A_{15}	235	216	0.55	0.92	0.37	86	0.44	0.05	0.39	91

Table 6.3 (*continued*)

Housing Projects	Total Units (N)	Occupied by White Tenants					Occupied by Black Tenants			
		Total	T_w	P_{wj}	DIFF'$_{wj}$	DIFF'$_{wj}$*N	T_b	P_{bj}	DIFF'$_{bj}$	DIFF'$_{bj}$*N
A_{16}	174	0	0.55	0.00	0.55	96	0.44	1.00	0.56	98
A_{17}	163	161	0.55	0.99	0.43	71	0.44	0.01	0.42	69
A_{18}	224	0	0.55	0.00	0.55	124	0.44	1.00	0.56	126
A_{19}	188	183	0.55	0.97	0.42	79	0.44	0.02	0.42	78
A_{20}	194	186	0.55	0.96	0.41	79	0.44	0.03	0.41	79
A_{21}	218	132	0.55	0.61	0.05	11	0.44	0.39	0.05	11
A_{22}	121	98	0.55	0.81	0.26	31	0.44	0.19	0.25	30
A_{23}	203	0	0.55	0.00	0.55	112	0.44	1.00	0.56	114
A_{24}	206	187	0.55	0.91	0.35	73	0.44	0.08	0.36	74
A_{25}	450	440	0.55	0.98	0.42	191	0.44	0.02	0.42	189
Total	**4,797**	**2,654**	—	—	—	**1,866**	—	—	—	**1,875**

Note: Approximately 1 percent of units in the Chicago PHA were occupied by Hispanic and Asian tenants.

The total number of projects was 25. Since the names of individual housing projects were not available, these names have symbolically been replaced by A_n ($n = 1, 2, \ldots, n$).

First estimate of the index of racial segregation of tenants (I_{xpha}) is equal to 0.39.

Table 6.4
First Estimates of the Index of Racial Segregation in Elderly Housing in New Haven, 1977

Housing Projects	Total Units (N)	Occupied by White Tenants					Occupied by Black Tenants				
		Total	T_w	P_{wj}	DIFF'$_{wj}$	DIFF'$_{wj}$*N	Total	T_b	P_{bj}	DIFF'$_{bj}$	DIFF'$_{bj}$*N
A_1	23	22	0.69	0.96	0.26	6	1	0.30	0.04	0.26	6
A_2	36	17	0.69	0.47	0.22	8	19	0.30	0.53	0.22	8
A_3	60	30	0.69	0.50	0.19	12	30	0.30	0.50	0.20	12
A_4	65	61	0.69	0.94	0.24	16	4	0.30	0.06	0.24	16
A_5	108	88	0.69	0.81	0.12	13	19	0.30	0.18	0.13	14
A_6	40	35	0.69	0.88	0.18	7	5	0.30	0.13	0.18	7
A_7	116	93	0.69	0.80	0.11	12	23	0.30	0.20	0.11	12
A_8	80	47	0.69	0.59	0.11	9	33	0.30	0.41	0.11	9
A_9	96	44	0.69	0.46	0.24	23	52	0.30	0.54	0.24	23
A_{10}	18	9	0.69	0.50	0.19	4	9	0.30	0.50	0.20	4
Total	**642**	**446**	—	—	—	**109**	**195**	—	—	—	**110**

Notes: Total number of projects $N = 10$.

Estimate of the index of racial segregation of tenants (I_{xpha}) is equal to 0.17.

Table 6.5
Index of Racial Segregation in Elderly Housing in Washington, D.C., 1977

Housing Projects	Total Units (N)	Occupied by White Tenants					Occupied by Black Tenants				
		Total	T_w	P_{wj}	DIFF'$_{wj}$	DIFF'$_{wj}$*N	Total	T_b	P_{bj}	DIFF'$_{bj}$	DIFF'$_{bj}$*N
A_1	28	0	0.06	0.00	0.06	2	28	0.93	1.00	0.07	2
A_2	89	0	0.06	0.00	0.06	5	89	0.93	1.00	0.07	6
A_3	341	25	0.06	0.07	0.01	4	316	0.93	0.93	0.01	2
A_4	104	6	0.06	0.06	0.00	0	98	0.93	0.94	0.01	1
A_5	119	3	0.06	0.03	0.04	4	116	0.93	0.97	0.04	5
A_6	268	18	0.06	0.07	0.01	1	244	0.93	0.91	0.02	6
A_7	191	7	0.06	0.04	0.02	5	183	0.93	0.96	0.03	5
A_8	158	21	0.06	0.13	0.07	11	137	0.93	0.87	0.07	10
Total	**1,298**	**80**	-	-	-	**33**	**1,211**	-	-	-	**37**

Notes: Total number of housing projects $N = 8$.

First estimate of the index of racial segregation of tenants (I_{xpha}) is equal to 0.03.

ing projects, has been calculated only for PHAs with total 1980 population of 100,000 or more. The values of the estimates are shown in Table 6.6. Overall, the estimates were higher in the South and Midwest. Some differences between the values for blacks and whites are due to the presence of Hispanics and Asians, particularly in the Northeast and West.

Of the three groups of projects (family, elderly, and mixed family/elderly) the estimates tend to be highest for mixed family/elderly housing projects. There are, however, substantial variations among the regions in the level of racial segregation in family and elderly housing. In the Midwest, the estimates of the index of segregation in elderly housing were higher than in other regions.

Overall, the analysis indicates that in 1977 the South was not the lone bastion of racial segregation. While southern PHAs such as Roanoke, Virginia, and Atlanta had indices of racial segregation of tenants in family and elderly housing greater than 0.40, an even greater number of PHAs in the Northeast (e.g., Buffalo) and Midwest (e.g., Indianapolis) had similarly high indices of racial segregation of tenants. In the elderly housing program, the South had the highest proportion, 60 percent, of housing projects jointly occupied by white and black tenants;[10] this proportion was nearly as high, 57 percent, in the Northeast and West, but much lower, 41 percent, in the Midwest.

In family housing, the proportion of projects jointly occupied by white and black tenants was 73 percent in the Northeast and much lower at 54 percent, 48 percent, and 41 percent respectively in the Midwest, the South, and the West. In mixed elderly/family housing, the proportion of projects jointly occupied by white and black tenants was 73 percent in the Northeast and 66 percent in the South, but only 40 percent in the Midwest.

The concentration of whites in elderly projects and of nonwhites (particularly African-Americans) in family projects, evident in the 1977 data, contin-

Table 6.6
Estimates of the Index of Racial Segregation in Subsidized Low-Income Housing, 1977

Regions	Projects	First Estimates		Second Estimates	
		Whites	Blacks	Whites	Blacks
Northeast	1,893	0.16	0.19	0.39	0.29
Midwest	2,203	0.23	0.24	0.37	0.39
South	4,027	0.18	0.20	0.45	0.45
West	948	0.15	0.15	0.38	0.26
U.S.	**9,071**	**0.18**	**0.20**	**0.39**	**0.29**

Table 6.7
**Demographic Characteristics of Household Heads in
Subsidized Housing by Race, 1983**

	Age of Household Head			
Race of Household Head	<30 years (%) of race	30-49 years (%) of race	50-61 years (%) of race	62+ years (%) of race
White	18.1	20.2	11.7	50.0
Black	26.6	39.6	13.5	20.5
Total	**21.0**	**27.8**	**12.5**	**38.6**

Source: The *American Housing Survey* (National Files) 1983.

ues in the later American Housing Survey. In 1983, nearly 62 percent of white household heads but only 34 percent of black ones in public housing were over fifty years of age (see Table 6.7).

PATTERNS OF RACIAL OCCUPANCY IN 1992

By 1992 the Multifamily Tenants Characteristics System (MTCS) had been partially implemented by the Department of Housing and Urban Development.[11] The MTCS data cover approximately 50 percent of units in all federally assisted low-income housing programs, amounting to 832,118 units in 11,793 housing projects (this figure excludes Indian Housing Authorities units and those in overseas U.S. possessions such as Puerto Rico). The distribution of these units among various racial groups is shown in Table 6.8.

Table 6.8
Distribution of Units among Racial Groups

Regions	White	Black	Hispanics	Asian	Other	Total
Northeast	96,428	118,367	41,886	2,365	902	259,948
Midwest	97,166	95,474	3,993	3,412	4,587	204,632
South	77,646	197,395	24,927	999	646	301,613
West	33,236	22,119	23,481	11,543	3,082	93,461
U.S.	**304,476**	**433,355**	**94,287**	**18,319**	**9,217**	**859,654**

Source: U.S. Department of HUD, *Multifamily Tenants Characteristics System, 1992*.

Table 6.9
Assignment Index of Racial Segrega-
tion in Low-Rent Housing, 1992

Regions	White	Black	Hispanics
Northeast	0.14	0.18	0.13
South	0.12	0.14	0.05
Midwest	0.17	0.18	0.02
West	0.12	0.14	0.11
U.S.	**0.14**	**0.17**	**0.10**

Source: U.S. Department of Housing and Urban Development, *Multifamily Tenants Characteristics
System,* 1992.

Overall, 37 percent of the units were occupied by white tenants, 52 percent by black tenants, and 11 percent by Hispanics. In terms of the pattern of racial occupancy, Table 6.9 shows the values of the estimate $I'_{xpha(assign)}$ of the index of racial segregation, which are lower for the 1992 data than the estimates calculated from 1977 data (Table 6.6). The pattern was uneven across regions: the Northeast and Midwest had virtually the same levels of racial segregation initially in the two years, and the decline occurred almost entirely in the South and West.

A frequency count of housing projects in which no racial group of tenants predominates indicates that the South as a whole has more racially mixed housing projects than any other region, with 46 percent of all mixed housing projects. The Midwest accounted for another 30 percent of all racially mixed housing projects and the Northeast and West for 20 percent and 4 percent, respectively.

Racial occupancy data are available for 11,793 housing projects. Of these, 7,073 drew at least 80 percent of their tenants from one racial group, whites in 4,100 and blacks in 2,973. This subcategory includes 1,799 housing projects (15 percent of the total) occupied by tenants from only one racial group, blacks in 1,010 of them and whites in the other 789. Table 6.10 shows the distribution of these racially homogeneous housing projects by census region.

The incidence of racially homogeneous housing projects does not appear to be related to the size of the PHA, housing projects occupied exclusively by black tenants being found, for example, in Philadelphia and Chicago as well as such small cities as Milford, Connecticut, and Terre Haute, Indiana.

The size of PHA aside, the data indicate that blacks as a group tend to be more concentrated in high density projects (over 500 units) than whites. Twenty of New York City's thirty high density projects, for example, are predominantly or exclusively black, as are ten of Baltimore's eleven. (The pattern of

Table 6.10
Distribution of Racially Homoge-
neous Housing Projects by
Census Regions, 1992

Regions	Black	White	Total
Northeast	141	229	370
South	665	272	937
West	39	44	83
Midwest	165	244	409
U.S.	1,010	789	1,799

Source: U.S. Department of Housing and Urban Development, *Multifamily Tenants
Characteristics System,* 1992.

racial occupancy in New York City is noteworthy since this PHA has historically, since 1939, been one of the most integrated.) Boston is an exception to
this tendency; high density housing projects there are predominantly occupied by white tenants (see Table 6.11).

In Table 6.12 the values of the estimate $I'_{xn(\text{admit})}$ of the index of segregation
are shown for PHAs with a 1992 total population of 50,000 or more.

Unlike previous periods, the values of the 1992 admissions estimate are
lower than the values of the assignment estimate for black tenants. This is
essentially a distortion caused by the use of the share of each racial group in
households in the PHA as the criterion for equity. Since whites as a group
comprise a greater proportion of all households in most PHAs, the values are
heavily biased in favor of whites. Other distortions in the value of the index
may result from omissions in the still preliminary and partial MTCS occupancy data.

By census regions, the values of the second estimate appear to be higher for
both racial groups in the Midwest, where elderly housing is most concentrated,
and substantially lower in the South, where family housing predominates. This is
suggestive of some regional shift in the level of segregation, but without detailed
racial occupancy data by housing subsidy programs no definitive conclusion
about possible correlates of the pattern of occupancy can be drawn.

PATTERNS OF INCOME DISPERSAL

The data on subsidized housing dispersal are based on geography rather
than income areas, typically characterizing housing projects located in core
cities of large metropolitan areas as central-city projects and those located
outside core cities as noncentral-city projects (regardless of the demographic
or economic characteristics of the suburban municipalities included).

Table 6.11
**Pattern of Racial Occupancy in Housing Projects
with 500 or More Units, 1992**

PHA	Projects	Total	White	Black
Boston, MA	4	3,799	2,386	505
Hartford, CT	2	1,594	48	614
Baltimore, MD	11	7,710	742	6,830
New York, NY	30	35,401	4,274	17,989
Philadelphia, PA	10	7,506	67	6,837
Total Northeast	**57**	**56,010**	**7,517**	**32,775**
Birmingham, AL	4	2,399	12	2,383
Mobile, AL	3	1,544	59	1,475
Tampa, FL	3	1,621	103	1,385
Louisville, KY	6	4,500	675	3,719
New Orleans, LA	12	9,875	12	9,826
Nashville-Davidson, TN	6	3,765	722	3,019
San Antonio, TX	2	1,604	16	12
Dallas, TX	2	1,509	13	1,429
Richmond, VA	4	2,429	16	2,406
Total South	**42**	**29,246**	**1,628**	**25,654**
San Francisco, CA	2	2,552	243	1,615
Los Angeles, CA	6	4,418	90	2,051
Seattle, WA	4	2,808	568	1,045
Total West	**12**	**9,778**	**901**	**4,711**
Chicago, IL	15	12,226	192	11,775
Detroit, MI	2	1,596	33	1,553
Cincinnati, OH	3	2,629	66	2,555
St. Louis, MO	2	1,600	12	1,587
Total Midwest	**22**	**18,051**	**303**	**17,470**

Table 6.12
Admissions Index of Racial
Segregation in Low-Rent
Housing, 1992

Regions	White	Black
Northeast	0.16	0.13
South	0.12	0.13
Midwest	0.17	0.17
West	0.14	0.15
U.S.	**0.14**	**0.15**

Note: The values of the first estimate
of the index are shown separately in
Table 6.9.

Despite the limitations of the available data, some benefit can be gained from the examination of the distribution of housing projects among geographic areas. Historically, central-city subsidized housing projects were built in the low-income area.[12] This pattern of dispersal was a direct result of the use of low-rent housing as an instrument of the central business district reorganization and reclamation described earlier.[13] Moreover, until recently, the development of subsidized housing in noncentral-city areas was limited for both economic reasons such as land costs and political reasons such as the opposition by suburbanites to the location of housing projects (particularly prospectively black-occupied ones) in their neighborhoods.[14] Some municipalities blocked proposed low-rent housing projects by legislative moratoria on new subdivisions or by rezoning prospective housing project sites as open space and park. Nevertheless some subsidized housing, particularly for the elderly, has been constructed outside of central-city areas since about 1970.

Table 6.13 provides a partial understanding of where and when low-income housing projects were built between 1968 and 1974. The table summarizes the distribution of units for which the federal government provided annual subsidies for operation and amortization under the Annual Contribution Contract.

The first line indicates that of 57,229 units occupied in 1968, 44,063 were located in central cities and 13,166 units outside them. The other lines are similar. The distribution of units between the central city and noncentral city was most unequal in 1972 with only 9,670, or 20 percent, of the 48,899 units leased to tenants that year located outside the central city. Cumulatively, 311,388 subsidized housing units were leased to tenants between 1968 and 1974, of which 228,852 units (over 73%) were located in central-city areas and 82,536 units (26.5%) outside central-city areas.

Table 6.13
Dispersal of Public Housing Units Placed under
ACC, 1968–1974

Years	Total Units	In CC PHAs	%	In NCC PHAs	%	Index (D_n)
1968	57,229	44,063	77.0	13,166	23.0	0.27
1969	69,843	48,837	69.9	21,006	30.1	0.20
1970	64,553	49,174	76.2	15,379	23.8	0.26
1971	37,576	28,653	76.3	8,923	23.8	0.26
1972	48,899	39,229	80.2	9,670	19.8	0.30
1973	19,890	12,390	62.3	7,500	37.7	0.12
1974	13,398	6,506	48.6	6,892	51.4	0.01
Total	**311,388**	**228,852**	**73.5**	**82,536**	**26.5**	**0.23**

Source: U.S. Department of Housing and Urban Development, 1974.

Notes: ACC = Annual Contribution Contract; CC = central city; NCC = noncentral city.

Based on the assumed definition of income integration (an equal division of units between the two geographic areas), the estimate of the index of income separation in 1968 is 0.27 (see Table 6.13). Overall, for the period 1968–1974, the estimate D_s of the index of income separation is 0.23.

The distribution of the Section 8, Section 236, and Rent Supplement programs units among central-city and noncentral-city areas in 1977 is shown in Table 6.14.

For units with a known geographic location, the estimate D_n is

$$D_n = |0.71 - 0.50| = 0.21 \qquad (28)$$

SUMMARY

The analysis of the patterns of income and racial distribution of subsidized low-income housing shows continuing racial segregation, despite the adoption of the Civil Rights and Fair Housing Acts, and income separation, despite a relative decline in the concentration of housing projects in low-income central-city areas.

Between 1968 and 1974, over 73 percent of subsidized housing units leased to tenants were located in low-income areas. In 1981 and 1983, this proportion declined to 70 percent and 66 percent, respectively. This reflected to some extent significant variation by housing subsidy programs, inasmuch as

Table 6.14
Distribution of Units in the Section
8, Section 236, and Rent Supplement
by Geographic Areas, 1977

Geographic Location	Total Units	Percent of Total
Inside central city	3,103	0.38
Outside central city	1,266	0.44
Location not reported	2,645	0.18
Total All Areas	**7,014**	**1.00**

Source: U.S. Department of Housing and Urban
Development, tape file: *SHACO-236RS77
SORTED*.

71 percent of family housing units but only 58 percent of elderly housing
units were located in low-income areas in 1977.

The distribution of units among income areas also varied significantly by
race of tenants, with blacks as a group more likely than whites to live in
housing projects located in low-income areas. In 1981, 83 percent of black-
occupied units but only 60 percent of white-occupied units in the entire subsidized housing program were located in low-income areas. In the public
housing subprogram of the subsidized housing program, 76 percent of black-
occupied units and only 47 percent of white-occupied units were in housing
projects located in low-income areas that same year.

The estimates of the index of racial segregation show high levels of racial
segregation across PHAs in 1977. The estimate of the assignment index, which
measures the effect of the assignment of racial groups among housing projects,
was 0.20 for blacks in that year; in absolute terms, this would suggest that
216,811 public housing units would have had to be exchanged between blacks
and other racial groups to arrive at a racially neutral pattern of occupancy. In
the same year, the estimate was 0.18 for whites, indicating that, in absolute
terms, 195,130 units would have had to be exchanged between whites and
other racial groups to arrive at a racially neutral pattern of occupancy. By
regions, the value of the estimate of the index of racial segregation appears to
be highest in the Midwest, challenging the traditional image of the South as
the bastion of black–white segregation.

In addition to the separation of tenants by racial groups within PHAs, the
values of the admissions index, which measures the degree of racial discrimination in the access to subsidized housing, suggest the existence of racial

discrimination. In 1977 values for this index were 0.35 for black tenants and 0.39 for white tenants nationally, and higher in some regions—0.45 for both black and white tenants in the South, for example.

Data from the 1977 survey of PHAs indicate a concentration of racial minorities in family housing projects and of whites in elderly projects. That year, more than 51 percent of all family housing projects had their units occupied predominantly or exclusively by black tenants, and nearly 50 percent of all elderly housing projects had their units occupied predominantly or exclusively by white tenants. Extreme cases include Montgomery, Alabama, where family housing projects were occupied exclusively by black tenants and elderly projects exclusively by white tenants, and Livonia, Michigan, where elderly housing units (the only subsidized housing available in the PHA) were occupied exclusively by whites despite the presence of a substantial eligible black population.

The distinction between the elderly and family housing programs first began in 1956 with the introduction of elderly housing. Although the white population eligible for family housing is numerous and does not appear to be economically better off than the eligible black population, fewer and fewer nonelderly whites are choosing to live in subsidized housing. The long-term implication of this is that racial segregation in federally subsidized housing will likely be an enduring social problem.

NOTES

1. *Code of Federal Regulations, Title 3, 1959–1963 Compilation* (Washington, D.C.: U.S. Government Printing Office, 1964). Section 801 of the Fair Housing Act of 1968 directs HUD and local housing authorities to "administer the programs and activities relating to housing and urban development in a manner affirmatively to further" antidiscrimination and "fair housing." However, this statute provides practically no enforcement power. According to Congress, "any person who claim to have been injured by a discriminatory housing practice or who believes that he will be irrevocably injured by a discriminatory housing practice that is about to occur . . . may file a complaint with the Secretary. Complaints shall be in writing and shall contain such information and be in such form as the Secretary requires. Upon receipt of such a complaint the Secretary shall furnish a copy of the same to the person or persons who allegedly committed or are about to commit the alleged discriminatory housing practice" Public Law 90–284 (April 11, 1968) *United States Statute at Large* 82 (Washington, D.C.: U.S. Government Printing Office, 1969): 85–86.

2. Data from the 1977 survey of PHAs are cataloged in a file called CDBOUT in the HUD's T18 System. Data from the MTCS system were obtained, with the assistance of John Goering, from the Office of Public and Indian Housing, U.S. Department of Housing and Urban Development.

3. The 1977 occupancy data, however, are problematic in many respects. Some variables related to racial occupancy and center-city status are either inadequately coded or lack sufficient documentation. For 846 housing projects the total number of units coded as leased to tenants and employees is actually smaller than the sum of units coded as leased to all racial groups of tenants. In one housing project, for ex-

ample, the total number of units leased to white tenants who were the only tenants was coded as 400 units. But the total number of units leased to tenants and employees was only 40. For additional discussion of some methodological problems associated with the 1977 database, see A. Bickford and Douglas S. Massey, "Segregation in the Second Ghetto: Racial and Ethnic Segregation in American Public Housing, 1977," *Social Forces* 69, 4 (1991): 1011–1036.

4. Additional data on the race of tenants were collected by the Urban Institute in 1977. These data, unlike the 1977 data, are based on a survey of tenants rather than housing projects. The data were provided by the Department of Housing and Urban Development (from the CPT–T18 System). In 1979, data on the race of tenants in Section 8, Rent Supplement, and Section 236 housing subsidy programs were collected by the Department of Housing and Urban Development. The data (provided to the authors by HUD's CPT–T18 System) are cataloged under the name SHACO-236RS77 sorted.

5. Observations with all numeric variables coded with 9s were considered to be missing.

6. These are Arizona, Minnesota, Montana, Nevada, New Mexico, North Dakota, Oklahoma, South Dakota, and Wisconsin.

7. An alternative classification of units in the 1977 database, used by Bickford and Massey, was project ownership. Under this classification, housing projects were classified as authority owned if the project code was missing and subsidized if the project code was valid and not missing. See Bickford and Massey, "Segregation in the Second Ghetto," 1016.

8. Since the total number of units is not available by housing subsidy programs, the analysis of the pattern of racial segregation in individual programs like the Section 202/8, Section 236, or Section 8, is not possible through the use of this data file. This limitation of the data is significant because it means that the role of factors affecting household eligibility for a particular housing subsidy program (and the pattern of racial occupancy) cannot be examined in a significant detail.

9. In determining the total number of units used in the analysis, we excluded units administered by the Bureau of Indian Affairs and units in U.S. overseas possessions. In addition, the total number of units in housing projects with a coded, total number of units smaller than the sum of units leased to all racial groups of tenants, has been set equal to the sum of units leased to all racial groups. As a result, the effective size of subsidized low-income housing has been reduced to 1,084,055 units. Although the total number of units has not been adequately tabulated by housing subsidy programs, it appears, based on the meaning of the variable project code, that in addition to the conventional public housing for families (first authorized in 1937), units from other relatively more recent programs were also included.

10. It is assumed that tenants are not segregated by racial sections in biracial projects.

11. The system tracks information on the racial characteristics of tenants in federally assisted housing programs, including both programs such as public housing, Section 23 housing, and home ownership assistance programs like the Turkey III and Indian Mutual Help. Unfortunately, they do not include racial occupancy data for the major Section 8 programs. Currently, the MTCS is still incomplete; the most comprehensive racial occupancy data are for medium-size and large PHAs (those with more than about 500 units).

12. According to some writers, "local elites" in many northern cities "alarmed by the black migration, white suburbanization, urban blight and inner city decay, [took] advantage of urban renewal legislation to carry out widespread slum clearance in growing black neighborhoods next to business districts and key urban institutions. . . . As the result, projects were usually built on cleared land in or near ghetto neighborhoods, often only a few blocks from where the poor minority families originally had lived." See Bickford and Massey, "Segregation in the Second Getto," 1012.

13. According to the Task Force on Housing in Florida, "the suburbs have little subsidized housing due to a general opposition of suburbanites to locating low-income housing within their communities. They fear a decline in property values, an upsurge in crime, and other unfavorable conditions associated with the poor. These communities have fought against the establishment of public housing, and have practiced exclusionary zoning to prevent developers from constructing low-cost housing." Florida Governor's Task Force on Housing and Community Development, *Housing in Florida* 5 (1972): 36.

14. *Kennedy Park Homes Association, Inc. v. City of Lackawanna, New York*, 436 F. 2d 108–109 (2d Cir. 1970). See also, *United States v. City of Black Jack, Missouri*, 508 F. 2d 1179–1181 (2d Cir. 1974). In Cleveland, a permit to build a low-rent public housing project for blacks outside of the three predominantly black residential areas (Hough, Glenville, and Lee-Seville) was revoked by city officials. See *Maryann Banks et al. v. Ralph J. Perk, as Mayor of the City of Cleveland, et al.*, 341 F. 1178 (Dist. Ct. 1972). There were exceptions to this rule, however. In the early 1960s, some suburban jurisdictions took advantage of the program of urban renewal to "revitalize and beautify" their communities. See, for example, Harry W. Reynolds, "Population Displacement in Urban Renewal," *American Journal of Economics and Sociology*, 22, 1 (1963): 113–128.

7

Trends in Subsidized Housing Segregation

In this chapter, we conduct a statistical test of the impact, if any, of the civil rights and fair housing legislation of the 1960s on racial segregation and income separation in federally subsidized low-income housing.

Data limitations are a serious hindrance when comparing historical trends, since we are far from the ideal situation of conceptually consistent data on racial occupancy and income dispersal of federally subsidized housing projects collected both before and after the legislation. Instead, as indicated in previous chapters, relevant data have been patchily collected (especially in the early period) and further distorted by changes in the definition and selection of variables. This situation limits our analysis of trends in segregation.

TRENDS IN INCOME SEPARATION

In analyzing changes in the degree of income separation of subsidized housing projects over time, it should be noted that the distribution of housing projects among income areas in a community can change simply as a result of economic changes in the community. Deterioration or revitalization of the surrounding community can move a housing project from a moderate-to-high-income area to a low-income area and vice versa.[1] Income areas can also change as a result of natural disasters (e.g., earthquake, flood, fire) or such

large-scale activities as freeway construction. Many of the changes in the
distribution of subsidized housing projects among income areas cannot be
attributed to actions or policies specific to public housing.

Assuming nevertheless that changes in the distribution of housing projects
among income areas are caused entirely by the process of site selection for
new projects, Table 7.1 shows the values of the index D_n of income separation
for selected years. During the period 1932–1937, the Housing Division of the
Public Works Administration built 21,640 units in forty-nine housing projects.[2]
Economically, there was no variation in the distribution of these projects among
residential neighborhoods. As a result, the index D_n of income separation was
at its highest possible level, 0.50.

During the period 1937–1941, the United States Housing Authority built
100,807 additional units of public housing, all of them located in previously
low-income areas or on vacant sites. The index D_n thus remained at the maximum possible level, 0.50.

After 1956, public housing projects for elderly and handicapped households were built outside of central cities. The approximately 640,000 units of
federally subsidized housing in 1960 included a substantial number outside
of central city areas, the proxy for the low-income area.[3] The index accord-

Table 7.1
Trends in the Income Separation of Subsi-
dized Low-Rent Housing Projects, 1938–
1983

Year	Federal Housing Agency	Units	% in Low Income Area	Index (D_n)
1938	PWA	21,640	100	0.50
1941	USHA	100,807	100	0.50
1944	FPHA	762,539	–	–
1960	PHA	472,916	82	0.32
1969	HUD	640,403	77	0.27
1974	HUD	1,042,868	73	0.23
1977	HUD	1,135,378	76	0.26
1983	HUD	1,082,868	82	0.32

Note: Data on the income dispersal of housing projects
are not available for 1992.

ingly declined to 0.32, well below the maximum. After the civil rights and fair housing laws, the index declined further, to 0.23 in 1974, before returning to 0.32 in 1983 (the most recent value). This paralleled the movement of the central-city share of housing projects, which reached a low of 73 percent in 1974; that is, in that year, 27 percent of housing projects units were outside of central cities.

Although some family housing projects were built outside central cities in this period, the decline in measured income separation resulted primarily from the substantial development of elderly housing, nearly half of it outside of central cities. From 1970 to 1983, 388,276 (over 68%) of 570,989 new family housing units were located in the low-income area while only 262,832 (56%) of 471,879 new elderly housing project units were located in low-income areas (see Table 7.2).

For the historical comparisons, the values of index D_n of income separation were divided into two groups, those before 1969 and those after, and the equality of the means of the groups was evaluated with a t-test. The null hypothesis that the mean indices of income separation of federally subsidized housing

Table 7.2
Estimates of the Index of Income Separation in Family and Elderly Housing, 1937–1983

Income Area	1937 - 1969		1970 - 1983	
	Units	%	Units	%
Family Housing				
Low	296,207	0.74	388,276	0.68
High	104,572	0.26	182,713	0.32
Total	**400,779**	**1.00**	**570,989**	**1.00**
Index D_n	0.24		0.18	
Elderly Housing				
Low	145,363	0.61	262,832	0.56
High	94,261	0.39	209,047	0.44
Total	**239,624**	**1.00**	**471,879**	**1.00**
Index D_n	0.11		0.06	

Source: Goering and Coulibaly, 277.

Note: Units in moderate-high-income areas include units in rural PHAs.

Table 7.3
t-test of Equality of the Means of the Index of Income Separation Before and After 1969

Classification Categories	N of Cases	Mean	SEE
Group A (1938 - 1960)	3	0.44	0.103
Group B (1969 - 1983)	4	0.27	0.037
Variances	**T**	**DF**	**Prob > |T|**
Unequal	2.705	2.4	0.098
Equal	3.098	5.0	0.027
H_0: Variances are equal:	**F'=7.71**	**DF = 2 & 3**	**SEE = 0.131**

Note: DF is the degree of freedom for the statistics F, SEE is the standard error of the estimate.

projects was unchanged after the civil rights and fair housing legislation is rejected, albeit at a relatively low level of confidence. The test shows a statistically significant difference between the two group means (see Table 7.3).

This result would be more powerful under the assumption of equal variances of group means, but the folded F statistic indicates that this assumption is not supported by the data. Nevertheless, under the more probable assumption of unequal variances, the test shows a statistically significant difference between group mean indices of income separation at 0.10 level. Consequently, the data do suggest a reduced level of income separation of federal housing projects after the civil rights and fair housing legislation, contrary to the null hypothesis of an unchanged level of income separation, and the change in income separation patterns does not appear to be purely the result of random within-group variation in the data.

In sum, the development of an elderly housing program and the participation of suburban communities in Urban Renewal (which, under Title I of the 1949 Housing Act and Title II of the 1954 Housing Act, required the rehousing of some displaced families in subsidized units) produced a statistically significant reduction of the level of income separation. Whether this has continued is not clear, as the 1983 value is equal to the 1960 value.

TRENDS IN RACIAL SEGREGATION

This analysis of trends in racial segregation is based on incomplete data collected at different times using conceptually inconsistent definitions of *segregation* and *race*.

Before World War II, most public housing projects were occupied exclusively by tenants from the same race; the relatively few characterized as racially mixed included as many with separate racial wings as with randomly mixed tenants of different races.

During World War II, radical, if temporary, change in the objectives of subsidized housing programs strongly influenced patterns of racial occupancy of housing projects and data collection methodology.[4] The subsidized housing stock underwent tremendous expansion, from about 100,000 units in 1941 to nearly 800,000 in 1945. Although racial occupancy data are incomplete, it is clear the vast majority of war housing tenants were white. Blacks were largely relegated to permanent public housing, essentially that built or authorized before the war. Relatively more reliable racial occupancy data for these permanent projects were collected by the Race Relations Branch of the FPHA. Since this constitutes most of the data from which it is calculated, the index of racial segregation for this period is likely to be biased toward housing projects with relatively more black tenants.

After World War II, the public housing picture again changed significantly as temporary war housing projects, mostly occupied by whites, were liquidated or demolished and as many tenants, more of them white than black, became ineligible on the basis of income for continued occupancy of permanent projects. In a relatively short period, blacks and other racial minorities came to predominate in conventional public housing.

Between 1953 and 1964, racial occupancy data were collected somewhat systematically by the Race Relations Branch of the Public Housing Administration, but only for entire states, not individual housing projects or PHAs, and only for those states with *open racial occupancy*.

In the post-1964 period, racial occupancy patterns in federally assisted housing were strongly influenced by the concentration of white tenants in elderly housing, first authorized by Congress in 1956, and of black tenants in more traditional family housing. These data tend to be relatively more detailed and conceptually consistent with one another than earlier period occupancy data.

Despite their limitations, comparison of indices of racial segregation for the periods before and after the civil rights and fair housing legislation can yield some insights. In Table 7.4, the two estimates of the index of racial segregation of black tenants are shown for the period 1938–1992.

The data indicate that the level of racial segregation in public housing was highest during World War II. Between 1941 and 1944, the value of the admissions estimate of the index increased from 0.33 to 0.43. After World War II, the values of the index steadily declined until 1960, remained essentially constant through 1977, and declined again in 1992.

The value of the estimates $I'_{xn(\text{assign})}$ and $I'_{xn(\text{admit})}$ of racial segregation were classified into pre- and post-1969 groups and the equality of means of the two groups for each estimate was evaluated with a t-test (see Table 7.5).

**Table 7.4
Trends in the Racial Segregation of
Subsidized Low-Rent Housing Projects,
1938–1992**

Year	Housing Agency	Units	Estimates of Index	
			Assign	Admit
1938	PWA	21,640	0.24	0.37
1941	USHA	100,807	0.31	0.33
1944	FPHA	762,539	0.32	0.43
1954	PHA[a]	309,578	0.21	0.38
1960	PHA	261,093	0.18	0.33
1962	PHA	472,916	0.19	0.29
1977	HUD	1,135,378	0.20	0.29
1992	HUD	832,118	0.17	0.15

[a]Public Housing Administraton

The differences are not statistically significant, so that the null hypothesis of equality of group means cannot be rejected. The tests consequently support the hypothesis that the level of racial segregation of tenants in subsidized low-income housing was not significantly affected by the civil rights and fair housing legislation of the 1960s. The test of equality of group means remains insignificant for both estimates of the index of racial segregation.

The means of the first estimate of the index of racial segregation were 0.24 for the period 1938–1962 and 0.18 for the period 1977–1992 (see Table 7.5, First Estimate). The *t*-test shows no statistical difference between the two means and the null hypothesis cannot be rejected either under the assumption of equal variances or under the opposite assumption of unequal variances. The test suggests that changes in the mean value of the index can be attributed to random within-group variations in the underlying data.

The second estimate of the index of racial segregation was 0.35 for the period 1938–1962 and 0.22 for the period 1977–1992. Again the null hypothesis of equality of the two mean indices of racial segregation of tenants cannot be rejected.

Overall, the tests suggest that the civil rights and fair housing legislation of the 1960s had little statistical impact on racial segregation in subsidized low-income housing. It is possible that the introduction at about the same time of new housing subsidy programs designed to meet the needs of discrete demo-

Table 7.5
t-test of Equality of Group Mean Indices of Racial Segregation
in Low-Income Housing

Classification Categories	N of Cases	Mean	STD
First Estimates			
Group A: 1938-1962	6	0.24	0.060
Group B: 1977-1992	2	0.18	0.021
Variances	**T**	**DF**	**Prob > |T|**
Unequal	1.962	5.6	0.102
Equal	1.242	6.0	0.261
Equal Variances: F' = 8.13	**Prob > F' = 0.520**		
Second Estimates			
Group A: 1938-1962	6	0.35	0.048
Group B: 1977-1992	2	0.22	0.098
Variances	**T**	**DF**	**Prob > |T|**
Unequal	1.855	1.2	0.296
Equal	2.746	6.0	0.033
Equal Variances: F' = 4.10	**Prob > F' = 0.197**		

graphic groups (i.e., the elderly) undermined efforts to effectively desegregate existing housing projects as prescribed by the federal antidiscrimination legislation.[5]

SUMMARY

The analysis of trends in segregation indicates that the level of income separation in low-income housing declined significantly immediately after the civil rights and fair housing legislation of the mid to late 1960s. Patterns of racial occupancy of housing projects changed for a time from an almost complete separation of tenants by race to very modest levels of interracial housing.

Structurally, the change in the level of racial segregation was not uniform across census regions. During the pre–civil rights period, the level of racial segregation of tenants was lowest in the Northeast and Midwest and highest in the South. After the civil rights reforms of the 1960s, the level of segregation of tenants was highest in the Northeast and Midwest and lowest in the South and West. In some Northeast PHAs, including those of New York City and Philadelphia, there was a change from a relatively high degree of racial integration before the civil rights reforms to racial homogeneity afterwards. Segregation in the later period is generally by program, many family and elderly housing projects being occupied predominantly or exclusively by blacks and by whites respectively.

Housing projects were less concentrated in low-income areas during the post–civil rights period. This was primarily a result of significant construction of elderly housing outside of central cities. A comparison of the indices of income separation for family and elderly housing projects indicated that elderly housing was significantly less separated by income than family housing. The 1937–1969 index of income separation was 0.24 for family housing projects and 0.11 for elderly projects; the post-1969 values declined to 0.18 and 0.06 respectively.

NOTES

1. Often housing projects located in such areas were liquidated in the private housing market.

2. Not included are three additional housing projects located in Puerto Rico and the U.S. Virgin Islands.

3. See U.S. Housing and Home Finance Agency, Urban Renewal Administration, *Urban Renewal Project Characteristics* (Washington, D.C.: U.S. Housing and Home Finance Agency, September 1955); see also idem, *Annual Report* (Washington, D.C.: U.S. Housing and Home Finance Agency, 1963). The rehousing of displaced families was mandated by Title I of the 1949 Housing Act and Title III of the 1954 Housing Act.

4. According to some accounts, there were seventeen different agencies in charge of the war housing program before the institution of the National Housing Agency.

5. For a case study of how the conventional public housing for families in New Haven became predominantly black, see Ellen Gesmer, "Discrimination in Public Housing under the Housing and Community Development Act of 1974: A Critique of the New Haven Experience," *Urban Law Review* 13 (1977): 49–80; see also U.S. Department of Housing and Urban Development, Office of Policy Development and Research, *The Gautreaux Housing Demonstration: An Evaluation of its Impact on Participating Households* (Washington, D.C.: U.S. Department of Housing and Urban Development, 1980), 101–122.

8

Summary and Conclusion

From its beginnings during the Great Depression, federally subsidized low-income housing in the United States has rarely been a true welfare program. It has more characteristically been an adjunct to corporate city central business district redevelopment, serving as a receptacle for some of the residents displaced by the demolition of low-income or minority neighborhoods too close to CBDs (and sometimes as the official rationale for such demolition, as in the Atlanta and St. Petersburg projects described in Chapter 5); or a component of the industrial mobilization of World War II; or a way of subsidizing owners of private housing.

Federal programs have actually provided shelter to less than 10 percent of the eligible population at any point in time; the meager resources made available were completely inadequate to the scale of the problem. For example, in the 1930s about one-third of the population of the country was ill housed, but the fewer than 22,000 federally supported units that existed by 1936 (some still under construction) were not even enough to rehouse the more than 30,000 households displaced by federally supported clearance activities in 1932–1936.

Federally subsidized low-income housing in the United States has also exhibited pervasive patterns of racial segregation, both in acceptance of tenants and assignment to units and of income separation.

Before World War II, 43 of the 49 projects supported by the Public Works Administration and at least 236 of the U.S. Housing Authority's 261 were completely segregated racially, a few by means of racial sections within projects but most by admitting only tenants of a particular race. This segregation surely kept some whites as well as blacks from benefiting from the federally subsidized housing of the era.

Wartime public housing programs were segregated incidentally by being targeted to workers in defense industries which customarily discriminated against blacks and directly by deliberately excluding many of the blacks who did qualify even when units were available.

After World War II, antidiscrimination laws enacted by many localities outside the South led to reduced levels of segregation in the assignment of public housing units, at least for a time. However, the sustained removal of income-ineligible tenants, most of whom were white, greatly increased the proportion of blacks among public housing residents. Many of the remaining white tenants were elderly, and as separate public housing projects for the elderly became common after 1956 the older family projects became increasingly dominated by racial minorities, especially blacks. This trend became even more significant as new construction essentially ceased for family housing while elderly housing continued to be built and seems to extend to the sector of privately owned units subsidized by rent supplements.

These patterns can be quantified by means of the indices $I'_{xn(assign)}$ and $I'_{xn(admit)}$ of racial segregation, which measure racial disparities respectively in assignment of tenants to units and in acceptance from the general population. The first index $I'_{xn(assign)}$ had a nationwide value of 0.24 for the 1930s, increased to 0.32 during the war, gradually declined to 0.18 in 1960, 0.20 in the 1970s and 0.17 in 1992. The second index fluctuated much more, from 0.37 in 1938 to 0.33 in 1960 and then 0.29 and 0.15 in 1977 and 1992, respectively.

Income separation, the disproportionate siting of public housing in low-income areas instead of evenly or randomly across neighborhoods of different income levels, is hard to analyze because of the difficulties of geographically delineating the low- and the moderate-to-high-income areas and of locating projects in one or the other. Nevertheless, rough gauges of income separation may be obtained by making some assumptions. For the earlier period, we can assume that projects built in demolished slum areas and formerly industrial vacant sites were located in the low-income area. For the modern era, we assume that in the old core cities of metropolitan areas are low-income, other places moderate-to-high income. Under these assumptions an index D_s of income separation can be calculated. The values of this index reflect a fairly absolute income separation in the early period (e.g., $D_s = 0.50$, the maximum possible values, for the PHA program of the late 1930s), giving way to some "income integration" in the modern era (values of D_s ranging from 0.32 in 1969 down to 0.26 in 1977, but back up to 0.32 again for the most recent, 1992, data).

Comparing the values of these indices before 1965 with those since suggests that the civil rights legislation of that time had no significant effect on the level of racial segregation in federally subsidized housing.

The current picture of federally subsidized housing, then, is of a certain amount of rent subsidies to tenants of private landlords and of publicly owned housing characterized by a curious form of de facto segregation, by demographically targeted programs (whites in elderly housing, blacks in family housing) rather than by housing projects. Such structural patterns of segregation seem largely beyond the influence of the civil rights legislation of the 1960s.

Appendix

In Chapter 4 we derived two measures of the index of racial segregation in subsidized low-income housing, $I_{xpha(\text{assign})}$ and $I_{xpha(\text{admit})}$, and argued that the two estimates jointly capture the racial composition of individual housing projects and the allocation of units among racial groups. The first index, $I_{xpha(\text{assign})}$, measures the *assignment* by racial group of households on the waiting list to available units. The second index, $I_{xpha(\text{admit})}$, measures the *access* by racial group of households in need of housing assistance to the PHA's facilities. The first index was calculated by averaging the deviation ($DIFF_{xj(\text{assign})}$) of the *observed proportion* of tenants from racial group X in individual projects from the *expected proportion* derived from the PHA's waiting list. The second index was calculated by averaging the difference ($DIFF_{xj(\text{admit})}$) between the *observed share* of racial group X among all tenant households and the *expected share* derived from the underlying demand for housing assistance (see Chapter 4 and the discussion there).

In estimating $I_{xpha(\text{assign})}$ and $I_{xpha(\text{admit})}$ simplifying assumptions were made which could result in lower or higher calculated values of segregation. Indeed, the estimate $I'_{xpha(\text{admit})}$, for example, assumes that the need for low-income housing in a PHA is proportional to the racial composition of the general population. However, as other studies have shown, the racial composition of the PHA's population is not always the best predictor of the racial composition of the demand for low-income housing in that PHA. Often the need for subsidized housing assistance in a PHA is more acute among racial minorities than their proportion in the general population would otherwise indicate. To use, therefore, the proportion of racial groups in the general population as a proxy for the racial composition of the demand for low-income housing may understate the degree of racial discrimination in the admission process and hence the overall amount of calculated segregation.

To remedy this obvious bias, a third estimate of the index of racial segregation is suggested. The variable $DIFF'_{xj(admit)}$, which measures the deviation of the racial composition of tenants in individual projects from the racial composition of all households (tenants and nontenants) in the PHA's jurisdiction, is redefined by the following formula:

$$DIFF''_{xj} = |P_{xj} - t_{xj}| \tag{A-1}$$

In Equation A-1, t_{xj} is taken to be the PHA-wide proportion of African-Americans among tenants if this group received *at least* a share of housing units that is equal to their proportion in the total PHA population (tenants and nontenants). Otherwise, if the proportion of African-Americans in the PHA's total population is larger than their proportion among housing tenants, then t_{xj} is taken to be their proportion in the PHA's population. P_{xj} is the actual proportion of African-Americans among tenants in housing project j.

PHA-level index H_{xpha} of racial segregation associated with discrimination in access (H_{xpha}) is calculated from the redefined $DIFF''_{xj}$ by the following formula:

$$H_{xpha} = \frac{\sum_{j}^{M} N_j DIFF''_{xj}}{\sum_{j}^{M} N_j} \tag{A-2}$$

where N_j is the total number of units in housing project j, M is the total number of housing projects in the PHA, and $DIFF''_{xj}$ is as above.

The estimate H_{xpha} assumes that African-Americans, not whites, are the most likely victims of racial discrimination in the allocation of units.[1] National level values of the estimate are shown in Table A-1 for 1939–1992.

No index can capture the many nuances of segregation and discrimination in low-income housing. An alternative index, which treats as discrimination only cases where the black share of public housing is less than the black share in the population, tends to understate the total process of discrimination by assuming away even the possibility of discrimination against whites. This assumption means that this alternative index tends to understate total discrimination. It also tends to understate total discrimination because of the

Table A.1
Estimates of the Index of Racial Segregation
in Low-Income Housing, 1939–1992

Name of Housing Agencies	Initial Index	Modified Index
Housing Division of PWA (1938)	0.37	0.23
United States Housing Authority	0.33	0.26
Federal Public Housing Authority	0.43	0.30
Public Housing Administration	0.38	0.29
Public Housing Administration	0.33	0.19
Public Housing Administration	0.29	0.20
Housing and Urban Development	0.29	0.22
Housing and Urban Development	0.15	0.15

actual differential in need for public housing between races, augmenting the likely error. The two indices form a bracket around some likely true level of discrimination, one surely too high and one surely too low.

NOTE

1. The treatment of PHAs with no African-American tenants and PHAs with African-Americans overrepresented in low-rent housing is a bit problematic. One method of estimating the index is to include all PHAs in which African-American and white tenants were present and calculate the deviation of the proportion of blacks in individual housing projects from their proportion in the PHA's population. Under this method, the index will be the weighted average of the deviations (positive as well as negative) of the proportion of blacks in housing projects from their proportion in the population. The other method of calculating the index is to assume that the PHA-wide racial composition of tenants is a reasonable standard of unsegregated occupancy when blacks as a group are not underrepresented in a low-income housing and recalculate the index only when the proportion of black in individual housing projects is lower than their proportion in the PHA's population. When blacks as a group are not underrepresented in a housing project, the value of the index will default to the value based on the PHA-wide racial composition of tenants. The effect of this approach, which is adopted in this appendix, is to lower the value of the national index.

Selected Bibliography

Aaron, Henry J. *Shelter and Subsidies: Who Benefits from Federal Housing Policies?* Washington, D.C.: The Brookings Institution, 1972.

Abrams, Charles. *Forbidden Neighbors: A Study of Prejudice in Housing.* New York: Harper & Brothers, 1955.

————. "Living in Harmony; Mixed Housing, A Proving Ground." *Opportunity* (July 1946): 116–118.

Abt Associates Inc. *Codebook for the Annual Housing Survey Data Base.* Prepared by Louise Hadden and Mireille Leger. Cambridge, Mass.: Abt Associates, Inc., 1988.

Aronovici, Carol. "The Future of Negro Housing." *Opportunity* (December 1940): 378–379.

Asby, William M. "No Jim Crow in Springfield Federal Housing." *Opportunity* (June 1942): 170–171.

Bauer, Catherine. "The First Six Months of USHA." *Housing Yearbook* (1938): 1–9.

————. "We Face a Housing Shortage." *Housing Yearbook* (1937): 61–73.

Beatty, Clarence W. "Urban Redevelopment—What Is the Value of Vacant Land in Blighted Areas?" *Journal of Housing* (January 1947): 8–9.

Becker, Gary S. *The Economics of Discrimination*, 2d ed. Chicago: University of Chicago Press, 1957.

Berry, Brian I., and John D. Kassarda. *Contemporary Urban Ecology.* New York: Macmillan, 1977.

Bianchi, Suzanne M., Reynolds Farley, and Daphne Spain. "Racial Inequalities in Housing: An Examination of Recent Trends." *Demography* 19, 1 (1982): 37–51.

Bickford, A., and Douglas S. Massey. "Segregation in the Second Ghetto: Racial and Ethnic Segregation in American Public Housing, 1977." *Social Forces* 69, 4 (1991): 1011–1036.

Bingham, Richard D. *Public Housing and Urban Renewal: An Analysis of Federal–Local Relations.* New York: Praeger, 1975.

Blandford, John B., Jr. "The National Housing Agency." *Housing Yearbook* (1944): 21–26.

Brown, Ina C. *Understanding Other Cultures.* Englewood Cliffs, N.J.: Prentice Hall, 1963.

Burgess, Ernest W. "Residential Segregation in American Cities." *The Annals of the American Academy of Political and Social Sciences* 140 (1928): 105–115.

Burke, Paul. *Researcher's Guide to HUD Data: With Notes on Related Information Sources.* Washington, D.C.: Department of Housing and Urban Development, Office of Policy Development and Research, 1984.

Butler, Edmund B. "Race Relations and Public Housing." *Interracial Review* (March 1947): 38–40.

Cam, Gilbert A. "United States Government Activity in Low-Cost Housing, 1932–1938." *Journal of Political Economy* (June 1938): 357–368.

Congressional Budget Office. *Federal Housing Assistance: Alternative Approches.* Washington, D.C.: U.S. Government Printing Office, 1982.

———. *Federal Housing Policy: Current Programs and Recurring Issues.* Washington, D.C.: U.S. Government Printing Office, 1978.

———. *Federal Subsidies for Public Housing: Issues and Options.* Washington, D.C.: U.S. Government Printing Office, 1983.

———. *The Housing Finance System and Federal Policy: Recent Changes and Options for the Future.* Washington, D.C.: U.S. Government Printing Office, 1983.

———. *The Long-Term Costs of Lower-Income Housing Assistance Programs.* Washington, D.C.: U.S. Government Printing Office, 1979.

Courant, Paul N. "Racial Prejudice in a Search Model of the Urban Housing." *Journal of Urban Economics* 5, 3 (1978): 329–345.

Courant, Paul N., and John Yinger. "On Models of Racial Prejudice and Urban Residential Structure." *Journal of Urban Economics* 4, 3 (1977): 272–291.

Deutsch, Morton, and Mary Evans Collins. *Interracial Housing: A Psychological Evaluation of a Social Experiment.* Minneapolis: University of Minnesota Press, 1951.

———. "Interracial Housing: A Survey of Opinion Among Housing Officials." *Journal of Housing* (January 1950): 14–16, 24.

Du Bois, W. E. B. "The Migration of Negroes." *The Crisis* (June 1917): 63–66.

———. "The Negro Artisan." In *Report of a Social Study Made under the Direction of Atlanta University; Together with the Proceedings of the Seventh Conference for the Study of the Negro Problems, Held at Atlanta University, May 27, 1902.* Edited by W. E. B. Du Bois. Atlanta: Atlanta University Press, 1902.

———. "Three Centuries of Discrimination Against the Negro." In *Minority Problems in the United States: A Textbook of Readings in Intergroup Relations.* Edited by Arnold M. Rose and Caroline B. Rose. New York: Harper & Row, 1965.

Ebenstein, William. "The Law of Public Housing." *Minnesota Law Review* 23, 7 (1939): 879–924.

Eliot, Sumner. "The Labor Movement and the Negro During Reconstruction." *Journal of Negro History* 33, 4 (1948): 429–430.

Ellison, Ralph. *The Invisible Man.* New York: Vintage Books, 1947.

Embree, Edwin R. "Balance Sheet in Race Relations." *The Atlantic Monthly,* May 1945, 87–89.

Emmerich, Herbert. "Public Housing in 1941." *Housing Yearbook* (1942): 10–19.

―――. "Public Housing in 1943." *Housing Yearbook* (1944): 27–46.

Epstein, Benjamin R., and Arnold Foster. "Discrimination in Housing." In *Minority Problems in the United States: A Textbook of Readings in Intergroup Relations.* Edited by Arnold M. Rose and Caroline B. Rose. New York: Harper & Row, 1965.

Evans, Orrin C. "Gains Made in Housing to Improve Racial Amity." *Philadelphia Record,* 26 February 1946.

Evans, William L. "Federal Housing Brings Residential Segregation To Buffalo." *Opportunity* (December 1942): 106–110.

―――. *Race Fear and Housing in a Typical American Community.* New York: National Urban League, 1946.

Farley, Reynolds. "Black–White Housing Segregation in the City of St. Louis: A 1988 Update." *Urban Affairs Quarterly* 26, 3 (1991): 442–450.

―――. "Residential Segregation of Social and Economic Groups among Blacks, 1970–80." In *The Urban Underclass.* Edited by Christopher Jenks and Paul E. Peterson. Washington, D.C.: The Brookings Institution, 1991.

Farrell, Thomas F. "Object Lesson in Race Relations." *New York Times Magazine,* 12 February 1950.

Federal Housing Administration. *The Underwriting Manual.* Washington, D.C.: Federal Housing Administration, 1938.

Federal Works Agency, Office of the General Counsel. *Lanham Act as Amended to July 15, 1943.* Prepared by Minnie Wiener, Librarian Law Library. Washington, D.C., 1943.

Federal Works Agency, United States Housing Authority. "Equivalent Elimination of Unsafe or Insanitary Dwellings." *Bulletin No. 3 on Policy and Procedure,* 15 April 1940.

Fisher, E. M., and L. Winnick. "A Reformulation of the Filtering Concept." *Journal of Social Issues* 7 (1951): 47–58.

Fleisher, Richard Stuart. "Subsidized Housing and Residential Segregation in American Cities: An Evaluation of the State Selection and Occupancy of Federally Subsidized Housing." Ph.D. diss., University of Illinois at Urbana–Champaign, 1979.

Florida Governor's Task Force on Housing and Community Development. *Housing in Florida* 5. Tampa, 1972.

Foley, Raymond N., John Taylor Egan, and Nathaniel S. Keith. *Statement on the Relationship of the Slum-Clearance and Low-Rent Housing Programs.* Washington, D.C.: U.S. Housing and Home Finance Agency, 1950.

Foner, Philip S., and Ronald L. Lewis, eds. *The Black Worker: A Documentary History from Colonial Times to the Present,* Vol. 4, *The Black Worker during the Era of the American Federation of Labor and the Railroad Brotherhood.* Philadelphia: Temple University Press, 1979.

"FPHA Rents." *FPHA Bulletin* 52 (September 1943).

Franklin, John Hope. "History of Racial Segregation in the United States." In *Promises to Keep: A Portrayal of Nonwhites in the United States*, Vol. 2. Edited by Bruce A. Glasrud and Alan M. Smith. New York: Rand McNally, 1972.

———. "The Negro Since Freedom." In *The Comparative Approach to American History*. Edited by C. Vann Woodward. New York: Basic Books, 1968.

———. "The Two Worlds of Race: A Historical View." In *The American Negro*. Edited and with an introduction by Talcott Parsons and Kenneth B. Clark and with a foreword by Lyndon B. Johnson. Boston: Houghton Mifflin, 1966.

Frazier, E. Franklin. "The Negro's Vested Interest in Segregation." In *Race Prejudice and Discrimination*. Edited by Arnold M. Rose. New York: Alfred A. Knopf, 1951.

Friedman, Lawrence M. "Public Housing and the Poor: An Overview." *California Law Review* 54 (1966): 642–649.

Galster, George C. *Black and White Preference for Segregation*. College of Wooster: Urban Studies Papers, September 1979.

Gans, Herbert J. "Human Implications of Current Redevelopment and Relocation Planning." *Journal of the American Institute of Planners* (February 1959): 15–25.

Gesmer, Ellen. "Discrimination in Public Housing Under the Housing and Community Development Act of 1974: A Critique of the New Haven Experience." *Urban Law Review* 13 (1977): 49–80.

Goering, John M., and Modibo Coulibaly. "Investigating Public Housing Segregation: Conceptual and Methodological Issues." *Urban Affairs Quarterly* 25, 2 (1989): 265–297.

Gordon, David M. "Capitalist Development and the History of American Cities." In *Marxism and the Metropolis: New Perspectives in Urban Political Economy*. Edited by William K. Tabb and Larry Sawers, 2d ed. New York: Oxford University Press, 1984.

Green, Rodney D. "Industrial Transition in the Land of Chattel Slavery: Richmond, Virginia, 1820–1860." *International Journal of Urban and Regional Research* 8, 2 (1984): 238-253.

Grob Gerald N. "Organized Labor and the Negro Worker, 1865–1900." *Labor History* 1, 2 (1960): 164–176.

Harvey, David. *The Urbanization of Capital: Studies in the History and Theory of Capitalist Urbanization*. Baltimore: Johns Hopkins University Press, 1985.

Hoch, Charles. "City Limits: Municipal Boundary Formation and Class Segregation." In *Marxism and the Metropolis: New Perspectives in Urban Political Economy*, 2d ed. Edited by William K. Tabb and Larry Sawers. New York: Oxford University Press, 1984.

Holleb, Doris B. "A Decent Home and Suitable Living Environment." *The Annals of the American Academy of Political and Social Sciences* 435 (1978): 102–111.

"Homes Project Finds Answer to Racial Issues." *New York Herald Tribune*, 13 February 1942.

Horne, Frank S. "War Homes in Hampton Roads." *Opportunity* (July 1942): 200–205.

"Housing Awaits Workers in Some Localities." *FPHA Bulletin,* no. 51 (September 1943).

"Housing Negroes and Other Minority Group War Workers in Region IX: A Memorandum from Robert Taylor, NHA and Frank Horne, FPHA (November 21, 1942)." Records of the Public Housing Administration (Project Files). RG 196, National Archives, Civil Reference Branch, Textual Records Division, Washington, D.C.

Hovde, B. J. "Negro Housing in Pittsburgh." *Opportunity* (December 1938): 356–358.

Hoyt, Homer. *The Structure and Growth of Residential Neighborhoods in American Cities.* Washington, D.C.: Federal Housing Administration, 1939.

Hughes, Langston. "Merry-Go-Around." *Common Ground* (Spring 1942): 27.

International Encyclopedia of the Social Sciences. 1972 ed., s.v. "Social Problem."

Jenkins, William S. *Pro-Slavery Thought in the Old South.* Chapel Hill: University of North Carolina Press, 1935.

Johnson, Charles S. "The Economic Status of Negroes." In *Summary and Analysis of the Materials Presented at the Conference on the Economic Status of the Negro, Held in Washington, D.C., May 11–13, 1933, under the Sponsorship of the Julius Rosenwald Fund.* Prepared by Charles S. Johnson. Nashville: Fisk University Press, 1933.

———. *Patterns of Negro Segregation.* New York: Harper & Brothers, 1943.

———. "Some Aspects of Negro Migration." *Opportunity* (October 1927): 297–299.

———. *To Stem This Tide: A Survey of Racial Tension Areas in the United States.* New York: Pilgrim Press, 1943.

Johnson, Charles S., Herman H. Long, and Grace Jones. *The Negro War Worker in San Francisco: A Local Self-Survey.* A project financed by a San Francisco citizen, administered by the YMCA, and carried out in connection with the race relations program of the American Missionary Association, Dr. Charles S. Johnson, Director, and the Julius Rosenwald Fund (San Francisco) 1944.

Johnson, Donald N. "Housing for Low and Moderate Income Families: Needs, Programs and Developments." In *Housing Problems in Oregon, Innovative Study Series. Report No. 1, Bureau of Governmental Research and Service.* Eugene: University of Oregon, nd.

Johnson, Ernest E. "Public Houser No. 1." *Opportunity* (November 1942): 324–345.

Johnson, Gerald W. "Baltimore Might Make It." *The New Republic* (April 1966): 12–22.

Kain John F. "America's Persistent Housing Crises: Errors in Analysis and Policy." *The Annals of the American Academy of Political and Social Sciences* 465 (1983): 136–148.

Kain, John F., and John M. Quigley. *Housing Markets and Racial Discrimination: A Microeconomic Analysis.* New York: National Bureau of Economic Research, 1975.

Katznelson, Ira. *City Trenches: Urban Politics and the Patterning of Class in the United States.* New York: Pantheon, 1981.

Laurenti, Luigi. *Property Value and Race: Studies in Seven Cities.* Berkeley and Los Angeles: University of California Press, 1960.

"The Lesson of Willow Run." *Task* (15 October 1943): 9–18.

Lieberson, Stanley. "An Asymmetrical Approach to Segregation." In *Ethnic Segregation in Cities.* Edited by Ceri Peach, Vaughan Robinson, and Susan Smith. Athens: University of Georgia Press, 1981.

Litchfield, Electus D. "Yorkship Village in 1917 and 1939." *The American City* 54, 11 (1939): 42–43.

Locklear, William R. "The Celestials and the Angels: A Study of the Anti-Chinese Movement in Los Angeles to 1882." *Southern California Quarterly* 62 (1960): 239–256.

Long, Herman H., and Charles S. Johnson. *People v. Property: Race Restrictive Covenants in Housing.* Nashville: Fisk University Press, 1947.

Longan, Elizabeth. "Progress by Local and State Agencies." *Housing Yearbook* (1938): 40–117.

"Majority of LHA Members are Bankers, Businessmen or Industrialists." *FPHA Bulletin* 4, 2 (1947).

Marcuse, Peter. "The Beginnings of Public Housing in New York." *Journal of Urban History* 12, 4 (1986): 353–390.

Marks, Carole. "Black Workers and the Great Migration North." *Phylon* (1984): 148–161.

Markusen, Ann R. "Class and Urban Social Expenditure: A Marxist Theory of Metropolitan Government." In *Marxism and the Metropolis: New Perspectives in Urban Political Economy.* Edited by William K. Tabb and Larry Sawers, 2d ed. New York: Oxford University Press, 1984.

Marx, Karl. *Capital: A Critique of Political Economy,* Vol. 1, Part 2. Moscow: Progress Publishers, 1978.

Maslow, Will. "Prejudice, Discrimination, and the Law." *The Annals of the American Academy of Political and Social Sciences* 275 (1951): 9–17.

"The Massacre of East St. Louis: An Investigation by the National Association for the Advancement of Colored People." *The Crisis* (September 1917): 219–238.

Massey, Douglas S., and Nancy A. Denton. "The Dimensions of Residential Segregation." *Social Forces* 67, 2 (1988): 281–315.

———. "Hypersegregation in U.S. Metropolitan Areas: Black and Hispanic Segregation along Five Dimensions." *Demography* 26, 3 (1989): 373–391.

McEntire, Davis. *Residence and Race.* Berkeley and Los Angeles: University of California Press, 1960.

———. *Special Research Report to the Commission on Race and Housing.* Berkeley and Los Angeles: University of California Press, 1960.

McGraw, Booker T. "Desegregation and Open Occupancy Trends in Housing." *Journal of Human Relations* (Fall 1954): 57–69.

McNair, William N. "Letter Addressed to the National Public Housing Conference from William N. McNair, Mayor, City of Pittsburgh." *Public Housing Progress* 1, 3 (1935): 3.

"More Housing to Help Meet Needs of Detroit Negroes." *FPHA Bulletin* 2, 3 (1944).

Morison Samuel. *The Oxford History of the American People.* New York: Oxford University Press, 1965.

Moron, Alonzo G. "Where Shall They Live? The Accommodation of Minority Groups in Urban Areas." *The American City* (April 1942): 67–71.

Moynihan, Daniel P. "Employment, Income, and the Ordeal of the Negro Family." In *The American Negro.* Edited and with an introduction by Talcott Parsons and Kenneth B. Clark and a foreword by Lyndon B. Johnson. Boston: Houghton Mifflin, 1966.

Muth, Richard F. "Residential Segregation and Discrimination." In *Patterns of Racial Discrimination; Volume I, Housing.* Edited by George M. von Furstenberg et al. Lexington, Mass.: Lexington Books, 1974.

Myrdal, Gunnar Karl. *An American Dilemma.* New York: Harper & Brothers, 1944.

National Advisory Commission on Civil Disorders. *Final Report.* Washington, D.C.: U.S. Government Printing Office, 1968.

National Association of Housing and Redevelopment Officials. *This Is Public Housing.* Washington, D.C.: National Association of Housing and Redevelopment Officials, 1988.

National Commission on Urban Problems. *Building the American City: Report of the National Commission on Urban Problems.* New York: Praeger, 1969.

National Committee Against Discrimination in Housing. *Citizens' Guide to the Federal Fair Housing Law of 1968.* New York: National Committee Against Discrimination in Housing, 1968.

National Housing Agency, Federal Public Housing Authority, Statistics Division. *Families in Low-Rent Housing: Data on Income, Rent, and Number of Persons in Families Reexamined for Continued Occupancy in Projects Constructed Under PL–412 and in PWA Projects January–June, 1944: Report S–550, Table 8.* Washington, D.C.: National Housing Agency, 1944.

National Housing Agency, Office of the Administrator. *Negro Share of Priority War Housing—Private and Public as of December 31, 1944.* Washington, D.C.: National Housing Agency, 1 May 1945.

National Housing Conference. *Housing Yearbook.* Washington, D.C.: U.S. Government Printing Office, 1965.

———. *Public Housing Tour Guide.* New York: National Housing Conference, 1940.

National Housing Law Project. *Subsidized Housing Handbook: How to Provide, Preserve and Manage Housing for Lower-Income People.* Berkeley: National Housing Law Project, 1982.

"The Negro's War." *Fortune* (June 1942).

"Negro Tenants in 110,000 Dwellings." *FPHA Bulletin,* no. 3 (September 1944).

Nesbitt, George B. "Relocating Negroes from Urban Slum Clearance Sites." *Land Economics* (August 1949): 275–288.

"New York Mayor, Business Men Demand Public Housing." *Public Housing Progress* (10 June 1936).

Nichols, Franklin. "Interracial Aspects of Public Housing." *Interracial Review* (November 1939): 169–171.

"Non-Discrimination Provisions Broadened." *FPHA Bulletin,* no. 4 (July 1943).

Parks, Robert. "The Bases of Race Prejudice." *The Annals of the American Academy of Political and Social Sciences* 140 (1928): 11–20.

Pettigrew, Thomas F. "Racial Change and Social Policy." *The Annals of the American Academy of Political and Social Sciences* 441 (1979): 114–131.

———. *Racially Separate or Together?* New York: McGraw-Hill, 1971.

Post, Langdon. "Race Relations Training Improves Management Job." *Journal of Housing* (June 1947): 172–179.

President's Conference on Home Building and Home Ownership. *Negro Housing: Report of the Committee on Negro Housing.* Washington, D.C.: U.S. Government Printing Office, 1932.

"Project Roll Call: A Review of Large-Scale Rental Housing Projects." *Housing Yearbook* (1939): 118–133.

"Public Housing." *The Architectural Forum* (May 1938): 345–349.

Public Housing Administration. Records of the Housing Division of PWA, 1933–1937. RG 196. "Application of Capitol Planning and Housing Corporation, Atlanta, Georgia, November 23, 1933," National Archives.

"Racial Friction Is Found Absent in Housing Unit." *Herald Tribune* (New York) 5 January 1946.

Ratcliff, R. V. *Urban Land Economics.* New York: McGraw-Hill, 1949.

"The Reorganization of Federal Housing Agencies." *Housing Yearbook* (1942): 1–9.

Reynolds, Harry W. "Population Displacement in Urban Renewal." *The American Journal of Economics and Sociology* 22, 1 (1963): 113–128.

Riis, Jacob August. *The Battle with the Slums*. New York: Macmillan, 1902.

———. *How the Other Half Lives: Studies among the Tenements of New York*. New York: Sagamore Press, 1957.

Roof, Wade Clark. "Race and Residence: The Shifting Basis of American Race Relations." *The Annals of the American Academy of Political and Social Sciences* 441 (1979): 1–12.

Rose, Arnold M. "Intergroup Relations v. Prejudice: A Pertinent Theory for the Study of Social Change." *Social Problems* 4, 2 (1956): 173–176.

———. "Theory for the Study of Social Problems." *Social Problems* 4, 3 (1957): 189–199.

Rubinowitz, Leonard S. *Low Income Housing: Suburban Strategies*. Cambridge, Mass.: Ballinger, 1974.

Russell Sage Foundation. *Negro Housing in Towns and Cities: 1922–1937*. New York: Russell Sage Foundation, 1937.

Schaller, Lyle E. "Urban Renewal: A Moral Challenge." *The Christian Century* 27 (January 1962): 805–807.

Shaffer, Helen B. "Slum Clearance: 1932–1952." *Editorial Research Report* 11, 20 (1952): 803–820.

Sims, Newell L. "Techniques of Race Adjustment." *Journal of Negro History* 16, 1 (1931): 79–87.

Spain, Daphne. "Race Relations and Residential Segregation in New Orleans: Two Centuries of Paradox." *The Annals of the American Academy of Political and Social Sciences* 441 (1979): 82–96.

"State and Local Activity." *Housing Yearbook* (1939): 1–102.

Sterner, Richard. *The Negro's Share: A Study of Income, Consumption, Housing, and Public Assistance*. New York: Harper and Brothers, 1943.

Steward Frank. "Christianity's Grass Roots Grow at Berea Homes." *The Cleveland Press*, 14 May 1945.

Strauss, Nathan. "Public Housing 1938–1939: From Plans and Policy into Projects." *Housing Yearbook* (1939): 103–114.

———. "Public Housing 1940–1941: A Review of the United States Housing Authority's Activities." *Housing Yearbook* (1941): 226–239.

Struyk, Raymond J., and Marc Bendick, Jr., eds. *Housing Vouchers for the Poor: Lessons from a National Experiment*. Washington, D.C.: Urban Institute Press, 1981.

"Subsidies for Housing." *The Architectural Forum* (April 1938): 309–316.

Taeuber, Karl E. "The Effect of Income Redistribution on Racial Residential Segregation." *Urban Affairs Quarterly* 4, 1 (1968): 5–14.

———. "Negro Residential Segregation: Trends and Measurements." *Social Problems* 12, 1 (1964): 42–50.

———. "Racial Segregation: The Persisting Dilemma." *The Annals of the American Academy of Political and Social Sciences* 422 (1975): 87–96.

"Tenant Policy Threatens Housing Program." *Public Housing Progress* (April 15, 1935).

Texas Advisory Commission on Intergovernmental Relations. *Public Housing in Texas: Past, Present and Prospective*. Austin: The Commission, 1974.

Thomas, William L. "The Psychology of Race Prejudice." *American Journal of Sociology* 9 (1904): 593–611.

United States Congress, Senate. Committee on Banking, Housing, and Urban Affairs. *Distressed HUD-Subsidized Multifamily Housing Projects.*" Hearings before the Committee on Banking, Housing, and Urban Affairs. 95th Cong. Washington, D.C.: U.S. Government Printing Office, 1977.

————. Committee on Education and Labor. *Creating a United States Housing Authority.* Hearings before the Committee on Education and Labor. 75th Cong., 1st sess. Washington, D.C.: U.S. Government Printing Office, April 14, 15, and May 11, 1937.

————. Committee on Education and Labor. *Slum and Low-Rent Public Housing.* Hearings before the Committee on Education and Labor. 74th Cong., 1st sess. Washington, D.C.: U.S. Government Printing Office, 1935.

————. Committee on Education and Labor. *Slum and Low-Rent Public Housing.* Hearings before the Committee on Education and Labor. 74th Cong., 1st sess. Washington, D.C.: U.S. Government Printing Office, 1937.

————. "Prohibiting Transportation of Strikebreakers in Interstate Commerce." Report (to accompany S. 2403), 75th Cong., 1st sess. Senate Report 821. Washington, D.C.: U.S. Government Printing Office, 1937.

————. "To Create a United States Housing Authority." Report (to accompany S. 1685), 75th Cong., 1st sess. Washington, D.C.: U.S. Government Printing Office, 1937.

U.S. Department of Commerce, Bureau of the Census. *Changes in Distribution of Manufacturing Wage Earners 1899–1939.* Washington, D.C.: U.S. Government Printing Office, 1933.

————. *Current Population Reports, Consumer Income: Poverty in the United States 1990.*" Series P–60, no. 175. Washington, D.C.: U.S. Government Printing Office, August 1991.

————. *Location of Manufactures 1899–1929: A Study of the Tendencies toward Concentration and toward Dispersion of Manufactures in the United States.* Washington, D.C.: U.S. Government Printing Office, 1933.

————. *Negroes in the United States 1920–1932.* Washington, D.C.: U.S. Government Printing Office, 1935.

U.S. Department of Housing and Urban Development, Office of Policy Development and Research. *Characteristics of Selected Federally Aided Low Income and Assisted Multifamily Housing, 1950–1984.* Washington, D.C.: U.S. Department of Housing and Urban Development, 1985.

————. *The Gautreaux Housing Demonstration: An Evaluation of its Impact on Participating Households.* Washington, D.C.: U.S. Department of Housing and Urban Development, 1980.

————. *Home-Ownership for Lower-Income Families: Section 235 (i) Basic Instructions: A HUD revised Handbook 4210.1.* Washington, D.C.: U.S. Department of Housing and Urban Development, 1975.

————. *Housing for the Elderly and Handicapped: The Experience of the Section 202 Program from 1959 to 1977.* Washington, D.C.: U.S. Department of Housing and Urban Development, 1979.

————. *Housing in the Seventies: A Report of the National Housing Policy Review.* Washington, D.C.: U.S. Government Printing Office, 1974.

————. *Progress Report on Federal Housing and Urban Development Programs, Report to the Subcommittee on Housing and Urban Affairs; Committee on*

Banking and Currency, United States Senate September 1969. Washington, D.C.: U.S. Department of Housing and Urban Development, 1969.

———. *Public Housing Agency Administrative Practices: Handbook for the Section 8 Existing Housing Program.* Washington, D.C.: U.S. Government Printing Office, 1979.

———. *Report to the Congress: Leased-Housing Programs Need Improvements in Management and Operation.* Washington, D.C.: U.S. Department of Housing and Urban Development, 1975.

———. *Statistical Yearbook.* Washington, D.C.: U.S. Government Printing Office, annual.

———. *Study of the Modernization Needs of the Public and Indian Housing Stock.* Prepared by Abt Associates Inc. Cambridge, Mass.: Abt Associates Inc., 1988.

U.S. Department of Labor, Bureau of Industrial Housing and Transportation. *War Emergency Construction: Report of the U.S. Housing Corporation,* no. 1. Washington, D.C.: U.S. Government Printing Office, 1919.

U.S. General Accounting Office. *Opportunity for Accelerating Construction and Reducing Cost of Low-Rent Housing.* Washington, D.C.: U.S. Government Printing Office, 1970.

U.S. Housing and Home Finance Agency. *Annual Report.* Washington, D.C.: U.S. Housing and Home Finance Agency, 1950.

———. *Annual Report.* Washington, D.C.: U.S. Housing and Home Finance Agency, 1952.

———. *Annual Report.* Washington, D.C.: U.S. Housing and Home Finance Agency, 1963.

———. *Families in Low-Rent Projects Reexamined for Continued Occupancy during Calendar Year 1956: Report 225.1.* Washington, D.C.: U.S. Housing and Home Finance Agency, 1957.

———. *Families Moving into Low-rent Housing: Report 226.1.* Washington, D.C.: U.S. Housing and Home Finance Agency, 1957.

———. *Federal Laws, Low-Rent Public Housing, the United States Housing Act of 1937 and Related Laws as Amended through October 15, 1964.* Washington, D.C.: U.S. Housing and Home Finance Agency, 1964.

———. *Low-Rent Public Housing, Planning, Design, and Construction for Economy.* Washington, D.C.: U.S. Housing and Home Finance Agency, 1950.

———. *Occupancy by Negroes Families in Low-Rent Housing by State as of December 31, 1963.* Quarterly Report No. 200.0. Washington, D.C.: U.S. Housing and Home Finance Agency, 1963.

———. *Relocation from Urban Renewal Project Areas.* Bulletin. Washington, D.C.: U.S. Housing and Home Finance Agency, 1960.

———. *Statistics on PHA Operations, Families in Low-Rent Projects: Report No. 225.1* Washington, D.C.: U.S. Housing and Home Finance Agency, 1957.

———, Office of the Administrator, Division of Slum Clearance and Urban Development. *Relocation of Families, Continental United States, through March 1954.* Washington, D.C.: U.S. Housing and Home Finance Agency, 1954.

———. *Relocation of Families, Continental United States, through September 1955.* Washington, D.C.: U.S. Housing and Home Finance Agency, Urban Redevelopment Administration, 1955.

———. *Summary of Local Redevelopment Programs.* Washington, D.C.: U.S. Housing and Home Finance Agency, Urban Redevelopment Administration, 1952.

————, Urban Renewal Administration. *Urban Renewal Project Characteristics.* Washington, D.C.: U.S. Housing and Home Finance Agency, 1955.

————, Urban Renewal Administration. *Questions and Answers on Relocation Payments.* Washington, D.C.: U.S. Government Printing Office, 1960.

U.S. Works Projects Administration. *Urban Negro Housing in North Carolina.* Published with the Assistance of North Carolina Committee on Negro Affairs, 1939–1940.

"Urban Housing: The Story of PWA Housing Division 1933–1936." *Bulletin,* no. 2 (August 1936).

Van Valey, Thomas L., Wade Clark Roof, and Jerome E. Wilcox. "Trends in Residential Segregation 1960–1970." *American Journal of Sociology* 82, 4 (1977): 826–844.

Warren, Elizabeth C. "The Dispersal of Subsidized Housing in Chicago: An Index for Comparisons." *Urban Affairs Quarterly* 21 (1986): 484–500.

————. "Measuring the Dispersal of Subsidized Housing in Three Cities." *Journal of Urban Affairs* 8 (1986).

Watson, Frank. *Housing Problems and Possibilities in the United States.* New York: Harper & Brothers, 1935.

Weaver, Robert C. *Habitation with Segregation: Address before the National Committee against Discrimination in Housing (May 19–20).* Edited and published by the National Committee Against Discrimination in Housing. New York: National Committee Against Discrimination in Housing, 1952.

————. "Housing in a Democracy." Reprint, Philadelphia 1946.

————. *The Negro Ghetto.* New York: Russell & Russell, 1948.

————. "The Negro in a Program of Public Housing." *Opportunity* (July 1938): 1–7.

————. "Negro Labor since 1929." *Journal of Negro History* 35, 1 (1950): 20–38.

————. "Poverty in America: The Role of Urban Renewal." In *Poverty in America: Proceeding of a National Conference Held at the University of California at Berkeley,* 26–28 February 1965. Edited by Margaret S. Gordon. San Francisco: Chandler, 1965.

————. "The Problem of Race Relations in Public Administration." *Opportunity* (July 1943): 108–110.

————. "Race Restrictive Housing Covenants." *The Journal of Land & Public Utility Economics* 20, 3 (1944): 183–193.

————. "Racial Minorities and Public Housing." In *Proceedings of the National Conference of Social Work.* New York: Columbia University Press, 1940.

————. "Racial Policy in Public Housing." *Phylon* (Second Quarter 1940): 149–161.

Wesley, Charles H. *Negro Labor in the United States 1850–1925.* New York: Vanguard, 1927.

West Virginia Bureau of Negro Welfare and Statistics. *Negro Housing Survey of Charleston, Keystone, Kimball, Wheeling, and Williamson.* Charleston: Jarrett Printing, 1938.

"When the USHA Buys Land." *The New Republic* (25 October 1939): 341–343.

White, Michael J. "The Measurement of Spatial Segregation." *American Journal of Sociology* 88, 5 (1983): 1008–1018.

————. "Racial and Ethnic Succession in Four Cities." *Urban Affairs Quarterly* 20, 2 (1984): 165–183.

Wiedenmayer, Gustave E. "A Businessman Views of Urban Renewal." *Housing Yearbook* (1964): 19–21.

Wilson, William Julius. *The Declining Significance of Race: Blacks and Changing American Institutions.* Chicago: University of Chicago Press, 1978.

Wolfinger, Raymond E., and Fred I. Greenstein. "The Repeal of Fair Housing in California: An Analysis of Referendum Voting." *American Political Science Review* 62, 3 (1968): 753–761.

Wolgemuth, Kathleen L. "Woodrow Wilson and Federal Segregation." *Journal of Negro History* 44, 2 (1959).

Wood, Edith Elmer. "The Costs of Bad Housing." *The Annals of the American Academy of Political and Social Sciences* 190 (1937): 145–150.

———. "Rents in PWA Housing Division Projects." *Public Housing Progress* (June 1937).

———. *Slums and Blighted Areas in the United States.* College Park: McGrath Publishing, 1935.

Wood, Elizabeth. "Tenant Selection in a Locally Operated Project." In *Managing Low-Rent Housing: A Record of Current Experience and Practice in Public Housing.* Chicago: National Association of Housing Officials, March 1939.

Woodbury, Coleman. *Costs of Slums and Blighted Areas.* Chicago: National Association of Housing Officials, bulletin no. 99.

Woodward, C. Vann. *Origin of the New South 1877–1913.* Baton Rouge: Louisiana State University Press, 1951.

———. *The Strange Career of Jim Crow*, 2d ed. New York: Oxford University Press, 1966.

Woofter, T. J. *Negro Problems in Cities.* Garden City, N.Y.: Doubleday Doran, 1928.

Yinger, John. "A Note on the Length of the Black–White Border." *Journal of Urban Economics* 3 (1972).

Zorbaugh, Harvey W. "Urban Growth and Urban Planning." In *Public Housing Management: A Course of Lectures Offered by the New York University Division of General Education in Cooperation with the Municipal Service Commission and the New York Housing Authority.* New York: New York University Library, 1938.

Index

ABOUT THE AUTHORS

MODIBO COULIBALY is a Research Assistant in the Department of Economics at Howard University.

RODNEY D. GREEN is Professor of Economics at Howard University. His earlier books include *Minority Displacement and Rapid Transit Station Site Development* (1993) and *Forecasting with Computer Models: Energy, Population, and Econometric Forecasting* (Praeger, 1985).

DAVID M. JAMES is on the faculty at Howard University.

ISBN 0-275-94820-X

90000>

EAN

9 780275 948207

HARDCOVER BAR CODE